JEFFERSON:
A Monticello Sampler

❧ RICK BRITTON ❧

JEFFERSON:
A Monticello Sampler

⚜ RICK BRITTON ⚜

MARINER
PUBLISHING

BUENA VISTA, VIRGINIA

1 3 5 7 9 10 8 6 4 2

Library of Congress Control Number: 2005929332
Jefferson
A Monticello Sampler
Rick Britton
Includes Bibliographical References

p. cm.
1. Jefferson, Thomas, 1743–1826 2. Presidents—United States 3. Presidents—United States—Biography 4. United States History—18th century 5. United States History—19th century 6. United States History—Virginia, colonial period

I. Rick Britton, 1952— II. Title.

ISBN 13: 978-0-9768238-7-2 (softcover : alk. paper)

ISBN 10: 0-9768238-7-X

Cover Design: Chris Johnson (Mr. Visions) ♦ Book Design: Patty Williams

Mariner Publishing
A division of
Mariner Companies, Inc.
131 West 21st ST.
Buena Vista, VA 24416
Tel: 540-264-0021
www.marinermedia.com

Printed in the United States of America

This book is printed on acid-free paper meeting the requirements of the American Standard for Permanence of Paper for Printed Library Materials.

The Compass Rose and Pen are trademarks of Mariner Companies, Inc.

DEDICATION

This book is dedicated to the four ladies who have made my life worthwhile: my mother, Catalina, who brought me into this world and nurtured me; my beautiful wife, Victoria, without whose love and support nothing would be possible; Mia, my lovely and kind-hearted daughter-in-law; and my darling granddaughter Savannah, the light of my life.

Contents

List of Images

Foreword

If the Ages of European Renaissance and Reason converge, it is in America, in the lives of two men, one urban, one rural: Benjamin Franklin and Thomas Jefferson. Cosmopolites in a country of provincials—neither parochial, and both intellectually dazzling—they together perhaps best embody the promises of the famous Declaration that both worked on: life, liberty, and the pursuit of happiness. Although the wide-ranging curiosity, extensive travels, and important political and social contributions of each have been explored countless times, and doubtless will be reexamined endlessly for generations to come, fresh inquiries into the lives of these two fascinating American revolutionaries are always welcome. In this remarkable series of essays, Rick Britton explores the brilliance of Jefferson, from the vantage point of Monticello, his beloved home in Albemarle County, Virginia.

Without question, Thomas Jefferson was a genius. His wide-ranging interests included not only politics and government, for which he is best known, but architecture, education, languages, mathematics, cryptography, and the whole scope of Natural History and Natural Philosophy, which in his day encompassed archaeology, botany, paleontology, anthropology astronomy, meteorology, agriculture, and other physical sciences. His broad and unrestrained inquisitiveness did not go unrecognized by his contemporaries who for seventeen consecutive years elected him president of the illustrious scholarly organization that Franklin founded in the year of Jefferson's birth, the American Philosophical Society. It is thus daunting to embrace the whole Jefferson.

In the essays that follow, Rick Britton delves into Jefferson's unbounded curiosity, and his forays into Jefferson's life and world reveal much about his seemingly eclectic nature. There is much here about Jefferson's interest in the western expansion of the United States, not just the Lewis and Clark Expedition but the lesser-known exploration of the Ouachita River by William Dunbar and George Hunter and the subsequent twenty-four-man "Grand Excursion" into Louisiana, led by Thomas Freeman and Peter Custis in 1806. Of similar interest was Jefferson's search for possible relatives of the *Mastodon americanus*, which Jefferson imagined were roaming with the abundant buffalo, elk, and deer in Indian territory, near Big Bone Lick, Kentucky.

Likewise, there is much about Jefferson's incredible architectural legacy, with its Palladian influence, an impressive array of both private and public and buildings ranging from Monticello, Poplar Forest, Edgemont, Farmington, Oak Hill, and Barboursville, to the University of Virginia, the Virginia State Capitol, and the Buckingham, Botetourt, and other county courthouses. The author also chronicles the efforts to save Monticello and the emergence of the Thomas Jefferson Memorial Foundation.

There is a curious centrality of localness in these essays, and the writer never strays far from Monticello. Take, for instance, Jefferson's efforts to see Tuscan immigrant Filippo Mazzei—physician, merchant, horticulturist, and vintner—transplanted to a farm adjacent to Monticello. Or Lafayette's emotional visit to Jefferson in November 1824, an episode eagerly anticipated by Jefferson's neighbors but generally overlooked by historians. The author vividly portrays life on the Monticello plantation, not only as it was in the "Big House" but also in the cottages and workshops on the slave street known as Mulberry Row. He details the failed attempt of Albemarle native Edward Coles to enlist Jefferson to speak out against slavery, and Coles's move to Illinois in 1819 to experiment with emancipation and his subsequent election as governor. Britton reminds us that Jefferson had his embarrassments, and they too were sometimes linked to Monticello. We see Virginia's famous governor scampering away from his beloved Monticello as Banastre Tarleton's Green Dragoons occupied nearby Charlottesville in late spring 1781.

The magnitude of Jefferson's talent, energy, and achievement eclipses his complexity and contradictions, but for Britton all are subjects for scrutiny. Hence he reminds us that Thomas Jefferson had his weaknesses as well as his strengths. Jefferson was a complicated person with a darker side and the author does not whitewash the Sage of Monticello, for despite his flaws, Thomas Jefferson deserves the praise often lavished on him.

Rick Britton is a writer and historian, radio and television personality, photographer, and accomplished cartographer. He has his own voice and he writes with grace and finesse. His style is at once easy to read—journalistic or popular—yet grounded in solid and thorough research. The results of his jaunts into the past are for the reader insightful and delightful vignettes of one of America's most extraordinary individuals. This is a book of gems.

Frank E. Grizzard, Jr.
Lexington, Virginia

Preface

Thomas Jefferson was, and still is, an endlessly fascinating individual. He was a philosopher, a statesman, a scientist, an architect, as well as an early proponent of western expansion and public education. His was a life spent busy. Both modern political parties attempt to claim him, and pundits, reporters, and talking heads quote him virtually every day. One could spend an entire lifetime simply studying his life.

Living in Charlottesville, Virginia, for a good number of years—within sight of Monticello—I have countless times stumbled across anecdotes about the great man which immediately sparked my curiosity. I just had to know more. When I learned, for example, that Jefferson had convinced an Italian vintner—Filippo Mazzei—to take up residence nearby and ply his trade here in Albemarle County, I wanted to know how that came about. Who was Mazzei? Did the project succeed? Did Mazzei remain in central Virginia?

During the American Revolution, Lieut. Col. Banastre Tarleton, the notorious British cavalry commander, led a raid against Charlottesville in order to capture the state government (which had skedaddled here because the capital, Richmond, had fallen to the enemy). Jack Jouett supposedly rode overnight from Louisa to warn the legislators and then-exiting Governor Jefferson. Is that story true? Is it true that Jefferson just barely escaped capture? Legend has it that Tarleton's men apprehended a few of the assemblymen including Daniel Boone, who was here representing a section of Kentucky. Is that tale merely a legend?

Edward Coles—the second governor of Illinois and an influential abolitionist—was born in Albemarle County in 1786. Is it true that he corresponded with Jefferson regarding slavery? What were their letters like? In 1824 the sixty-seven-year-old Marquis de Lafayette visited Jefferson at Monticello during his grand tour of the nation. How long was he here? What was his reception like at the fledgling University of Virginia?

The answers to my many questions, naturally, just begat more questions. What were Jefferson's accomplishments within the confines of his native county of Albemarle (aside from designing Monticello and U.Va.)? How many realms of science was he heavily involved in? What was the Big Bone Lick Expedition? How many exploring parties did Jefferson dispatch into the Louisiana Territory? What was Central College? How many houses did Jefferson design? How did the Thomas Jefferson Memorial Foundation get started?

When I started writing, these queries—and their intriguing answers—became my story ideas. Lucky for me, I found editors who were interested in my essays and encouraged me to write more. The chapters of this book—independent, stand-alone pieces—began as articles that appeared in a number of central Virginia publications. They have all been re-edited and re-worked—most of them have been greatly expanded.

I want to take this opportunity to thank the many wonderful editors I have had the pleasure to work with over the years—Jamie Miller, Hillary Swinson, Mary Sproles-Martin, Kathleen Valenzi, Frank Grizzard, and Robert Viccellio.

Rick Britton
Charlottesville, Virginia
May 12, 2008

The beautifully winding Rivanna River.

(Photo by the author.)

1

THOMAS JEFFERSON:
Albemarle County's Favorite Native Son

For over one hundred years following Jamestown's settlement in 1607, Virginia's central Piedmont—beneath the gaze of the beautiful Blue Ridge—remained virtually a wilderness. Game was plentiful and the land was lush and fertile. Deer wandered the hilly countryside in large numbers, along with bears, elk, and even bison. Geese and ducks noisily paddled the ponds, while pigeons roosted in such a multitude—according to local tradition—that large tree limbs were broken down. Fat shad and herring swam the mountain-fed streams and rivers. The low grounds along those watercourses, as noted Andrew Burnaby, a visitor in the mid-1700s, were "exceedingly rich, being loam intermingled with sand." Higher up into the country, toward the mountains, he wrote, the value of the land—consisting of a deeper clay—only increased. Indian corn and tobacco grew easily, while grapes, strawberries, mulberries, chestnuts, and rattlesnake root appeared "wild and spontaneously." The forests were filled with myrtles, cedars, firs, dogwoods, red-flowering maples, sassafras-trees, and eight varieties of oak. "[O]ne may reasonably assert," he remarked, "that no country ever appeared with greater elegance or beauty."

White settlers began advancing into the central Piedmont, via the waterways, in the 1720s. (Mysteriously, the region's natives, the Monacan Indians and their contributor tribes, had retreated to the southwest some two generations earlier.) As the population grew in this frontier district jurisdictions were created. Goochland County—a vast tract straddling the James River and running west to the Blue Ridge—was formed in 1728. Albemarle County was sliced from Goochland in 1744. The area's first land patents were taken out in the late 1720s by some of Tidewater Virginia's most prominent families (although few of these principal grantees actually occupied their holdings). Many of these acquisitions were truly massive: George Hoomes of Caroline County, for example, obtained 3,100 acres while Nicholas Meriwether set claim to over 13,700. In 1730 John Carter, secretary of the colony, acquired 9,350 acres between the James and Hardware rivers. The law required that, in order to perfect the title to the acreage, a certain percentage of it had to be cleared and cultivated. This work was done primarily by slaves and tenant farmers—the advance guard, so to speak, of European settlement.

The Piedmont witnessed a change by the mid-1730s, however, as more and more of the grants went to individuals intending to live on the land and farm it themselves. One of these was Peter Jefferson, a rather large and inordinately strong man of Welsh ancestry. His eldest son, writing in 1821, referred to him as "the third or fourth settler, about the year 1737, of the part of the county in which I live." Peter Jefferson had had but a superficial education, but, according to his son, "being of a strong mind, sound judgment and eager after information, he read much and improved himself. . . ." The elder Jefferson's first land grant in the region was dated June 14, 1734. He later increased his Albemarle County property—in the eastern section known as "the Flatlands"—to approximately 3,000 acres, including valuable Rivanna River bottomland and a very attractive hillock: a spur of the Southwest Mountains. Legend has it that Peter Jefferson purchased the acreage upon which he built Shadwell, the family home, for the sum total of a bowl of arrack punch.

Thomas Jefferson was born at Shadwell—in what was then still Goochland County—on April 13, 1743. (The date on the calendar at the time, however, was April 2. Eleven days were added in 1752 when England and her colonies adopted the Gregorian calendar.) Sitting atop a gently sloping hillside several hundred yards north of the Rivanna, the original family home was but a small wooden affair. By the time Thomas was in his teens, however, the now-enlarged house sat in the midst of an impressive number of plantation outbuildings. On the river, within view, Peter Jefferson had a water mill. More importantly, however, just to the north of the homesite passed Three Notched Road—the central Virginia thoroughfare that stretched from Richmond to the Shenandoah Valley. From his earliest memory, therefore, Thomas Jefferson was connected simultaneously with the wilds of the frontier and the urban attractions of civilization.

In his 1821 *Autobiography*—which unfortunately he never completed—Thomas Jefferson commented, with pride, on his father's achievements. Though self-educated, Peter Jefferson, wrote Thomas, "was chosen with Joshua Fry[,] professor of Mathem[atics] in W[illiam] & M[ary] college[,] to continue the boundary line between Virginia & N[orth] Carolina. . . ." This surveying work was completed in 1749 when Thomas Jefferson was only six years old. The following year the colonial governor appointed Fry and Peter Jefferson to survey and illustrate a new map of the Old Dominion. Thomas called the resulting Fry-Jefferson map, published in 1751, the "1st map of Virginia which had ever been made, that of Capt. [John] Smith being merely a conjectural sketch." But Peter Jefferson, who died in 1757, was more than just a Piedmont planter turned surveyor and mapmaker. He was also a sheriff, justice of the peace, lieutenant colonel of the local militia, and represented Albemarle County in the House of Burgesses. It was an impressive legacy of public service, especially considering that Peter Jefferson only lived to be fifty.

This legacy, no doubt, helped propel Thomas Jefferson onto the public stage, for indeed public service—to which he devoted over thirty years—eventually emerged as his apparent "raison d'être." A citizen's public duty, as can be imagined, was one of his favorite topics. "There is a debt of service due from every man to his country," Jefferson penned in 1796, "proportioned to the bounties which nature and fortune have measured to him." As he was given much in the way of bounties, in other words, much also could be asked from him. "Some men are born for the public," he wrote to James Monroe in 1803. "Nature by fitting them for the service of the human race on a broad scale, has stamped them with the evidences of her destination and their duty." Jefferson, of course, was destined to stride ever so prominently across the national stage. But though his services to Virginia and the nation were many, and kept him away from his home a large portion of his life, he made numerous significant contributions to Albemarle County—the mountainous expanse he called "the Eden of the United States."

Education and hard work, naturally, were the building blocks of his achievement-filled life. Jefferson learned, at an early age, to apply himself rigorously to every task at hand. At age five he began his studies at an "English School" at Tuckahoe, a plantation perched above the James but a few miles west of Richmond. From age nine until he was sixteen Jefferson studied Greek, Latin, and French under the Reverends William Douglas—"a clergyman from Scotland [who] was but a superficial Latinist"—and James Maury, "a correct classical scholar. . . ." From 1760 until 1762 Jefferson attended the College of William and Mary, an institution historian Dumas Malone called the continent's pre-eminent "school for statesmen." It was there, in Williamsburg, the colonial capital, that Jefferson fell under the wonderful influence of mathematics professor William Small—"a man profound in most of the useful branches of science." There, too, Jefferson read the law under George Wythe, perhaps the colonies' finest legal scholar. "Mr. Wythe continued to be my faithful and beloved Mentor in youth," noted Jefferson in his *Autobiography*. "In 1767, he led me into the practice of the law . . . at which I continued until the revolution shut up the courts of justice."

Thomas Jefferson's career as a public servant began shortly thereafter. In 1768, the twenty-five-year-old Jefferson was elected by Albemarle's freeholders as one of their two representatives in the colony's influential House of Burgesses. He took office in Williamsburg in May of 1769. The year 1769, coincidently, marked the commencement of work on Jefferson's home, Monticello. Discussed in detail below, work on the mountaintop mansion would take up close to forty years. In 1772 Jefferson married a young widow—Martha Wayles Skelton—and it was to the still-embryonic Monticello that he brought her. Jefferson continued as a member of the House of Burgesses until 1775. His authorship of the Declaration of Independence the following year he considered his proudest accomplishment. He later laid out his purposes in penning the document as: "Not to find out new principles, or new arguments . . . but to place before mankind the common sense of the subject, in terms so plain and firm as to command their assent, and to justify ourselves in the independent stand we are compelled to take. . . . [I]t was intended to be an expression of the American mind. . . . " While serving in the Virginia legislature—from 1776 to 1779—Jefferson laid the groundwork for the eventual abolition of several of the state's ancient systems, including "primogeniture," the exclusive right of inheritance that had, since feudal times, been coveted by first-born males. He also established, for Virginians, the beginnings of a public school system and complete religious freedom. "As a result," noted Malone, Jefferson began "to appear on the page of history as a major prophet of intellectual liberty and human enlightenment."

Jefferson's two years as wartime governor of Virginia—1779 to 1781—were fraught with controversy and disappointment. The British invaded the state in force in 1781, and Governor Jefferson and the Legislature skedaddled from Richmond, the new capital, in order to avoid capture. Setting up shop temporarily in Charlottesville, the entire government of Virginia—including, unfortunately, the then-exiting governor—was forced to flee again when a British raiding force drew near. (This story is covered in detail in another chapter.) It was the low-point of Thomas Jefferson's political career. And a horrible time of personal tragedy. On September 6, 1782, Martha, his wife of ten years, died from the complications of childbirth. Jefferson remained in a grief-ridden "stupor of mind" until mid-October. (The ten-year marriage had produced six children, only two of whom—Martha, nicknamed Patsy, and Maria, called Polly—lived into adulthood. Only Patsy, unfortunately, outlived her father.)

Public service, with all of its day-to-day minutia, was demanding work, but for Jefferson it was also curative—it focused his mind away from life's sorrows and gave his life meaning. Following the end of the Revolution in 1783, Jefferson wrote the draft for Virginia's constitution and was briefly a member of Congress. He served as minister to France from 1785 to 1789, then as our nation's first secretary of state until 1793. Jefferson's service as vice president under President John Adams—1797 to 1801—included his authorship, anonymously, of the Kentucky Resolutions, one of the first delineations of States' Rights theory. Elected third president of the United States in March of 1801—following a painfully long deadlock with Aaron Burr in the House of Representatives— Jefferson was the first chief executive inaugurated in Washington, a city he had helped plan. During his first term, the Jefferson administration reduced the national debt, orchestrated the purchase of Louisiana from Napoleon—thus virtually doubling the country's size—and dispatched the Meriwether Lewis and William Clark Expedition, along with several others, to officially take the new territory's measure. (Jefferson's vision for the West, and the Freeman and Custis Expedition are covered in two subsequent chapters.) Jefferson's second term, however, was not so impressive. Although he maintained U.S. neutrality while Europe was ripped apart by the Napoleonic Wars, Jefferson countered the seizure of American ships and seamen with the disastrous Embargo Act of 1807. Eventually repealed in 1809, this isolationist policy was nonetheless extremely detrimental to American farmers and merchants.

At the end of his eight-year presidency, Thomas Jefferson remained in Washington City only long enough to assemble his papers, pack his bags, and witness his lifelong friend James Madison inaugurated as his successor. Departing the capital on March 11, 1809, Jefferson ferried across the Potomac and took the road to Albemarle County and retirement. Jefferson's central Piedmont friends had expressed an interest in meeting him enroute and escorting him into Charlottesville. These included, daughter Patsy had written, "Not only the militia companies but the body of the people. They wish it as the last opportunity . . . of giving you a public testimony of their respect and affection." Distaining both ceremonies and military courtesies, Jefferson begged off, writing that "It is a sufficient happiness to me to know that my fellow citizens of the county generally entertain for me the kind sentiments which have prompted this proposition. . . . I can say with truth that my return to them will make me happier than I have been since I left them."

The journey home—due to the weather and bad roads—took four days: "The last three days [of which]," he wrote, "I found it better to be on horse-back, and traveled eight hours through as disagreeable a snow-storm as I was ever in." Because of this exposure—and a few recent ailments that had troubled him—the sixty-five-year-old ex-president was at first worried about his health. At Monticello he recovered quickly from the fatigue of the trip, however, even though he noted that his "memory [was] not so faithful as it used to be." Be that as it may, Jefferson's Albemarle neighbors remembered all of the work he had done on their behalf. Indeed, during the seventeen-year retirement that lay before him, he continued to make his mark on his native region. There's no doubting that in Albemarle County Jefferson's footprints were—and remain to this day—indelible.

The first impression had been made even before Jefferson became a lawyer. Albemarle's early economy was completely dominated by one cash crop—tobacco. The Tidewater gentry who journeyed up the rivers into the Piedmont did so to replicate—on a grander scale—eastern Virginia society. That meant, among other things, growing the noxious weed. Planters would later complain of tobacco ruining their soil, but in early Albemarle land was plentiful. Growing tobacco was a relatively simple process—only an axe, plow, and hoe were needed—and the plant grew quickly and was dried quickly under the Piedmont sun. It grew best in the nutrient-laden soil of bottomlands and Albemarle County possessed many rich river valleys. As the tobacco economy took root, the need arose for organized transportation. Packed into large, sixty-gallon casks called hogsheads, the product had to be delivered to market, and in return the luxuries of civilization had to be hauled into the interior. Around 1740, a Piedmont circuit parson named Robert Rose had developed a way of lashing together two dug-out canoes in order to float tobacco down the James River. Capable of sustaining up to eight hogsheads, Rose's "tobacco canoes" encouraged Piedmont landowners to plant even more of their fields in tobacco.

Young Thomas Jefferson was naturally interested in waterborne commerce as the Rivanna River—which flows into the James twenty some miles downstream—bisected the 3,000 acres he had inherited from his father in 1764. But the river was rocky and treacherous to travel. "The Rivanna river had never been used for navigation," Jefferson later wrote, "scarcely an empty canoe had ever passed down it. Soon after I came of age I examined it's [sic] obstructions, set on foot a subscription for removing them[,] got an act of assembly [passed] & the thing effected, so as to be used completely & fully for carrying down all [of] our produce." The "act" referred to was passed in October of 1765 "for clearing the great falls of [the] James river [at Richmond] . . . and the north branch of [the] James river"—the Rivanna. It authorized the undertaking but left everything—the raising of the necessary funds and the dredging itself—up to the interested private parties. In the group of eleven trustees set up to receive subscriptions for the Rivanna River was the twenty-two-year-old Thomas Jefferson. "Locally he was the initiator of the project," wrote Malone, reflecting Jefferson's claim, "and probably the most active member of the group." Two hundred pounds were raised to make improvements on Albemarle's waterway. The river was surveyed and the channel eventually perfected by dredging and removing trees and large rocks. Proudly Jefferson later listed the endeavor as his first "service" to the public. In the 1780s—in his *Notes on the State of Virginia*—he described the Rivanna as "navigable for canoes and batteaux to its intersection with the South West Mountains, which is about 22 miles."

As noted above, Jefferson was elected in 1768 to represent Albemarle County's freeholders in the House of Burgesses. The twenty-six-year-old took he seat on May 8, 1769. Established in 1619, the House of Burgesses was the New World's first elective legislative assembly. (In England, a "burgess" was a representative of a borough seated in Parliament.) Although the House of Burgesses—which met twice annually—was empowered to enact colonial legislation, its efforts in that regard were subject to veto by the royal governor. "[D]uring the regal government, nothing liberal could expect success," Jefferson later wrote, summing up his experience as a burgess. "Our minds were circumscribed within narrow limits by an habitual belief that it was our duty to be subordinate to the mother country in all matters of government, to direct all our labors in subservience to her interests, and even to observe a bigoted intolerance for all religions but hers."

Jefferson retained his seat in the House of Burgesses—re-elected each year—until 1775. These years as an assemblyman were coincidental with growing tensions between the colonies and England. As a burgess Jefferson served on numerous committees but also put his signature to several "articles of association," public papers that declared that the House of Burgesses, not Parliament, had the sole authority to tax the colony of Virginia. In one such document, for example, the burgesses stated that they would neither import—nor after a specific date purchase—any items taxed by Parliament in order to raise revenue.

Jefferson's most valuable work during this period, however, was his authorship, in 1774, of the controversial *A Summary View of the Rights of British America*. Based on a set of resolutions adopted by Albemarle freeholders in July of that year, *A Summary View*, wrote historian Noble E. Cunningham, Jr., "presented a detailed enumeration of American grievances against both Parliament and the crown, formulating the list of charges that [Jefferson] would add to and incorporate into the Declaration of Independence." Virginia's ancestors, prior to coming to America, penned Jefferson in the piece, "were the free inhabitants of the British dominions in Europe, and possessed a right, which nature had given all men . . . of going in quest of new habitations, and of there establishing new societies, under such laws and regulations as to them shall seem most likely to promote public happiness. . . ." He argued that but a limited political connection remained between England and her North American colonies. "[O]ur emigration from England to this country gave her no more rights over us," he later wrote, "than the emigrations of the Danes and Saxons gave to the present authorities of [Denmark and Germany] over England." In *A Summary View* Jefferson denied the authority of Parliament, and also warned the king—whom he called "no more than the chief officer of the people"—that America's rights, far from being a royal gift, were "derived from the laws of nature." Well articulated, these extremely radical views were not shared by many others at the time, and placed him on the cutting edge of revolutionary thought. "Mr. Jefferson had the Reputation of a masterly Pen," John Adams wrote the following year of the backwater Virginian he met at the second Continental Congress. "He had been chosen a Delegate in Virginia, in consequence of a very handsome public Paper which he had written for the House of Burgesses, which had given him the Character of a fine writer."

Aside from being one of Albemarle's two burgesses, Thomas Jefferson acquired at least two other county titles. In 1770—the year after he took his seat in the House of Burgesses—the royal governor of Virginia, Lord Botetourt, named Jefferson lieutenant of Albemarle, overall head of the local militia. "Thus, at the age of twenty-seven," noted Malone, "he became the ranking official of his County and could be called Colonel. His service in this important post may not have been continuous, but he was occupying it when war actually broke out. . . ." At the commencement of the Revolution, Jefferson was retained by the now independent Virginia General Assembly as leader of the Albemarle County militia—a position that required no small amount of paperwork—and in 1777 he was listed as a local justice of the peace.

Thomas Jefferson's greatest Albemarle County legacies are his two local architectural masterpieces: Monticello and the University of Virginia. (Jefferson's founding and design of U.Va. is described in detail in another essay.) Work on Monticello—Italian for "hillock" or "little mountain"—had begun in 1769. The previous year the twenty-five-year-old Jefferson had contracted an Albemarle man to clear and level the mountaintop in preparation for the construction of his home and outbuildings. Its location was, and still is, truly remarkable. Chosen from the property inherited from Peter Jefferson, Monticello Mountain stands amongst the Southwest Mountains—albeit a shorter and more accessible member—alongside a large gap through which passes the Rivanna River. The fledgling town of Charlottesville, founded in 1762, sat within sight but two miles to the northwest. Twenty-five miles beyond, the majestic Blue Ridge Mountains command the horizon and mark the western extent of Albemarle County. If the view to the west was impressive, however, the panorama to the east was nothing short of spectacular. Stretching for just over fifty miles, the heavily forested vista—cut by a bright sliver of the Rivanna, rapidly flowing toward the James—contained but few evidences of the work of man. Jefferson called this his "sea view" because the sun, above the morning mist, appeared to be "rising as if out of a distant water."

First to go up on the "little mountain" was a small, two-story brick structure. Jefferson moved to this "home"—later named the "South Pavilion"—following the destruction of Shadwell, by fire, in 1770. "I have here but one room," he wrote the following year, "which, like the cobler's [sic] serves me for parlour [sic] for kitchen and hall. I may add, for bed chamber and study too." The main house—Monticello itself—was constructed in fits and starts, and was eventually forty years in the making. Monticello's first version, as shown in a detailed sketch by Jefferson from the early 1770s, featured only six rooms: a large central parlor on the main floor flanked by smaller rooms, one of these for dining; and above two bedrooms and a study. As he so enjoyed "putting up and pulling down," two smaller rooms were later attached and the parlor was enlarged. Ornamenting the home's portico, or entrance, were Ionic columns mounting Doric capitals. "The shell of the house was basically completed—certainly habitable—by 1784," wrote William L. Beiswanger, Monticello's director of restoration, "when Jefferson departed for France. . . . The evidence suggests, however, that he had not completed—perhaps not even begun—the interior finish work such as the moldings and plastering."

In design, Jefferson's "essay in architecture" was something completely new. One of the nation's first neo-classical homes, it ranked locally as "among the curiosities of the neighborhood." A self-taught architect, Jefferson eschewed Virginia's then-popular architectural style—Georgian—and turned instead to Italy for inspiration. In Monticello's conception he relied heavily on the works of Andrea Palladio, a sixteenth-century Italian who had carefully measured, and illustrated, what Jefferson called "the remains of Roman Grandeur." Using a later edition of Palladio's *Four Books of Architecture*, first published in 1570, Jefferson created, atop his idyllic mountain setting, a wonderfully accurate monument to the ancient world. And his design ideas reached out from the main house, encompassing the entire mountaintop. During the 1770s he devised symmetrical L-shaped wings, partially dug into the hillside, which housed his outbuildings, or dependencies, and connected his basement to two west lawn pavilions. Below the South Pavilion Jefferson established an orchard—with apple, pear, cherry, and peach trees—and further down the hillside he planted pomegranates, figs, and walnuts. For his lawn he ordered shrubbery. The forest that ringed his mountaintop clearing he preserved as "an asylum for wild animals," wrote Malone, "and he was already thinking of procuring a buck-elk to be monarch of the wood."

Over the years, the various improvements made to the Monticello plantation—both agricultural and structural—benefited the residents of Albemarle County. Just prior to the Revolution, for example, Jefferson assisted an Italian entrepreneur, Filippo Mazzei, in the establishment of a vineyard at Colle, on Monticello's southeastern slopes. Jefferson believed that the United States could "make as great a variety of wine as are made in Europe," and that Albemarle County possessed the "soil, aspect, and climate of the best wine countries." Although Mazzei's project eventually failed, the Italian vintner and his Tuscan laborers had nonetheless introduced into the central Piedmont their unique implements, as well as Italian wines and vegetables. In 1757, Peter Jefferson had built a mill at Shadwell, "drawing the water," noted Thomas Jefferson Wertenbaker, "by means of a canal from a dam a half-mile up stream." Everything was swept away by the great freshet of 1771. After the Revolution, Thomas Jefferson built at Shadwell, continued Wertenbaker, "a toll mill for the grinding of his own and his neighbors' grain, a sawmill, and a manufacturing flour mill. The last named was sixty feet by forty, was three stories high, and cost $1,000." The flour produced was stuffed into hogsheads, rolled onto batteaux, and floated to market in Richmond.

Of the approximately 5,500 acres Jefferson eventually owned in Albemarle only about one-fifth were ever under cultivation. Sometime in the 1790s he began devoting much of this acreage to wheat. The "slovenly business of tobacco making" was ruining his soil—tobacco drained the earth of nitrogen, among other things— so in the mid-1790s he began making efforts to restore the nutrients. "[H]e adopted a seven-year schedule of crop rotation," wrote Lucia Stanton, "incorporating three years of the soil-improving legume, red clover, as well as wheat, rye, potatoes, and field peas." The Piedmont's small farmers, emulating Jefferson's example, according to William Minor Dabney, also "converted mainly to wheat growing. Travelers found that in 1796 the shift away from tobacco [in Albemarle County] was almost complete." Despite Jefferson's application of scientific farming, however, the income from the new cash crop—wheat—proved insufficient. In search of other money-making ventures, Jefferson set up a nailery on Mulberry Row, the 1,000-foot-long lane which runs along the mountaintop's eastern edge. (Described in detail in another essay, Mulberry Row housed the slaves who worked in the big house, and featured, like the nailery, a number of light industrial shops.) Employing young slave boys age ten to sixteen, the nail factory produced in 1794 upwards of eight thousand nails a day. Many of the Piedmont's wooden structures were pounded together with Monticello nails.

The limited income from farming also encouraged Jefferson to better organize his labor force—his enslaved African Americans—and brought to his attention some of the newly invented agricultural machines. One of these was a threshing machine patented in 1788 by Scotsman Andrew Meikle of East Lothian. While serving as George Washington's secretary of state, Jefferson asked Thomas Pinckney, who had just been made minister to England and was about to depart, to "procure a model of those parts of [Meikle's contraption] in which the principle of the machine consists, and a written description of the rest. . . ." Jefferson had a full-sized copy of the model made at Monticello by John H. Buck, a millwright and a skilled mechanic. Using horse power—and small enough to be portable from field to field—the thresher was first tested by Jefferson at his "riverfield" during the 1796 harvest. He later wrote that it was threshing over one hundred bushels a day, "with great success." Jefferson himself invented a mathematically perfected plow—his "moldboard of least resistance"—which, although never patented, attracted much attention both in the United States and abroad.

During his five years as American minister to France—1784 to 1789—Jefferson had become infatuated with the new French architecture. "Here I am, Madame," he wrote from France in 1787, "gazing whole hours at the Maison Quarree, like a lover at his mistress. The stocking weavers and silk spinners around it consider me a hypochondriac Englishman, about to write with a pistol the last chapter of his history. . . . While at Paris, I was violently smitten with the Hotel de Salm, and used to go to the Tuileries almost daily to look at it. . . ." The recently built Parisian town homes—or hotels—Jefferson admired were one-story structures featuring elaborately decorated "rooms of entertainment" with eighteen-foot-high ceilings. "[B]ut in the parts where there are bedrooms," he wrote, "they have two tiers of them from 8 to 10 feet high each, with a small private staircase." Some of them boasted new-fangled contrivances like skylights and flush toilets.

Jefferson initiated the reconstruction of Monticello in 1796, three years after he resigned his post as secretary of state. Using many of the design elements he had taken note of in Paris, he dramatically transformed his mountaintop home. "The upper story was removed," wrote Beiswanger, "the northeast front extended, and a new second level created for bedrooms within the height of the first floor." Whereas the first house had only five rooms on the main floor, the new Monticello contained eleven. Reached via narrow staircases, the new second story held four bed chambers arranged along the northeast front—with windows running almost to the floor—and a smaller southeast space Jefferson called the "Appendix." On the third floor were additional bedrooms, and above the first-floor parlor Jefferson's truly stunning octagonal "Sky Room"—his dome room featuring circular windows and an oculus skylight. "The plainness of the three bedrooms at this level," wrote Beiswanger, "do nothing to prepare one for the grandeur of this room." Built in 1800, this capstone to Jefferson's garden entrance—so familiar to Americans because of its appearance on the nickel—featured mars-yellow walls and a floor of true-grass green. Based on the Temple of Vesta in Rome, Monticello's dome was the first such structure on a house in the United States. Seeing Monticello as a work in progress in 1796, Irishman Isaac Weld predicted that eventually it would be "one of the most elegant private habitations in the United States." The same year the Duc de la Rochefoucauld-Liancourt was even more complimentary, saying that Jefferson's home "will certainly deserve to be ranked with the most pleasant mansions in France and England."

When completed in 1809—the year Jefferson retired from his two-term presidency—the final version of Monticello was over twice the size of the first. The extra space proved useful. Jefferson had welcomed countless visitors to Monticello in previous years, but nothing could prepare him for the throng that ascended the "little mountain" after 1809. "Monticello was overrun . . . during these years," wrote historian Merrill Peterson, "especially after the return of peace in 1815. In the summer months flocks of tourists came up from the low country. . . . Many stayed overnight. Monticello became a kind of tavern." This flock included well-wishers, gate-crashers, fellow scientists, Republicans and Federalists, professors and students, and foreign philosophers and dignitaries, as well as numerous local farmers and merchants. Many were merely gawkers, some just wanted to shake the hand that had penned the Declaration. (Helping the ex-president with this multitude was daughter Patsy, in 1809 she and a number of her children moved into Monticello with Jefferson. She took over the official functions of hostess.) The shear weight of numbers, of course, heavily burdened Jefferson and his family—but it also introduced Albemarle County to the nation and the world.

While the visitors found Monticello's exterior fascinating, typically they were dazzled by what was inside. Monticello's interior, wrote Jefferson, "contains specimens of all of the different orders. . . . The [Entrance] Hall is in the Ionic, the Dining Room is in the Doric, the Parlor is in the Corinthian, and the Dome in the Attic." Aside from the classical orders, the first-floor rooms were also brimming with art, artifacts, and curios. The eighteen-foot-high walls of the entrance hall were covered with maps of Virginia and the world's continents. The room also featured dozens of Native American items sent back by Lewis and Clark. Jefferson's art collection was scattered throughout. In the tea room sat terra-cotta busts of John Paul Jones, Benjamin Franklin, George Washington, and the Marquis de Lafayette. A set of paintings related to the discovery of America—images of Amerigo Vespucci, Christopher Columbus, and Sir Walter Raleigh—hung in the parlor.

French aristocrat Baron de Montlezun paid a visit to Monticello in 1816. No stranger to Virginia, as a sub-lieutenant of infantry Montlezun had participated in the 1781 Battle of Yorktown. "Extremely rare things are seen in [Monticello]," he wrote, "some of which could not be found anywhere else. . . . Two . . . very curious objects are: (1) An Indian picture representing a battle; it is on buffalo hide, about five feet square. . . . (2) A map, also on buffalo hide, six feet square, without the least defect. It represents a part of the course of the Missouri. . . . There is also a mammoth's tusk and an elephant's, with a tooth of the latter to show how it differs from those of the mammoth. . . . [T]he pictures and portraits which adorn the different rooms [include] "a dead man arising from the tomb to testify; the surrender of Cornwallis in October 1781, at Yorcktown [*sic*], in Virginia; Diogenes looking for a man; Democritus and Heraclitus, etc., etc., etc."

During his seventeen-year-long retirement, Thomas Jefferson only rarely traveled outside of Albemarle County and never again left the state of Virginia. "I am as happy nowhere else, and in no other society," he wrote, "and all my wishes end, where I hope my days will, at Monticello. Too many scenes of happiness mingle themselves with all the recollections of my native woods and fields, to suffer them to be supplanted in my affection by any other." Jefferson died at Monticello on July 4, 1826—the fiftieth anniversary, to the day, of the adoption of the Declaration of Independence. The Albemarle County Court, hearing of his passing, entered the following upon its records: "As a testimonial of respect for the memory of Thomas Jefferson, who devoted a long life to the service of his country, the principles of liberty, and the happiness of mankind . . . who, uniting to a native benevolence a cultivated philanthropy, was peculiarly endeared to his countrymen and neighbors, who were witnesses of his virtue: Resolved that this Court and its officers . . . will wear crepe on the left arm for thirty days, and will now adjourn."

Lieut. Col. Banastre Tarleton (1754–1833).

II

"TERROR AND CONFUSION":
Banastre Tarleton's Raid on Charlottesville

"At this period, the superiority of the army, and the great superiority of the light troops, were such as to have enabled the British to traverse the country without apprehension or difficulty, either to destroy stores and tobacco in the neighborhood of the rivers, or to undertake more important expeditions."

- Lieut. Col. Banastre Tarleton

From the ridge above Monticello, Thomas Jefferson trained his glass on the little town of Charlottesville. It was the warm morning of June 4, 1781—a Monday. Anxiously he scanned the streets. The Albemarle County Courthouse was plainly visible against the backdrop of lush woodland. Glancing up over the four-foot-long telescope, Jefferson gazed westward beyond Charlottesville. The majestic Blue Ridge seemed a fortress of security. But this was not a time of security; not for the Old Dominion and her protectors, not for the governing body of the state, and certainly not for Thomas Jefferson, just ending his term as governor.

A nimble adjustment brought into focus a group of figures near the Swan Tavern. He was surprised to see them posed calmly, seemingly unhurried. As he picked his way back down to Monticello he mentally organized the chores that remained. In mid stride Jefferson remembered his walking sword that lay on the ground next to his telescope. When he climbed back to retrieve it he stole another look through the glass. Gone was the group of gentlemen. In their place rode a knot of green-jacketed cavalrymen, British dragoons! Behind them another squad of enemies dismounted and entered the courthouse. Time had most certainly run out. Now Charlottesville would play host to perhaps the darkest hours of Virginia history.

In 1781, the Revolutionary War came to central Virginia and the sleepy little backwater town of Charlottesville. During the first four years of war, Virginia had been spared the ravages of British incursions. That changed dramatically in the first half of 1781. Coincidentally, the first six months of 1781 were the last months of Thomas Jefferson's second term as governor of Virginia. The invasion of the state, and particularly the raid on Charlottesville, became a black mark on Jefferson's record of public service and a long-lasting political weapon for his enemies. The recounting of Lieut. Col. Banastre Tarleton's raid on Charlottesville would haunt the "Sage of Monticello" for decades to come.

In 1780, the British prosecuted the American war in the southern states to great success. They raided at will and more importantly won victories in the field, but not without long casualty lists. Parliament greeted the news of the Guilford Court-House, North Carolina success with the retort that another such "victory" would cost England the campaign. As 1780 came to a close the British, having generally ravaged North and South Carolina, turned their attention to the Old Dominion. "[T]he British cabinet . . . had changed its plan of operations," wrote Henry "Light Horse Harry" Lee (over thirty years later), "in the expectation of wresting from the Union its richest though weakest division. In pursuance of this system, the breaking-up of Virginia was deemed of primary importance. . . . "

Governor Thomas Jefferson understood the vulnerability of Virginia. The Atlantic and Chesapeake coasts granted easy access to the powerful Royal Navy, and the many navigable rivers offered unobstructed highways into the interior. In the fall of 1780 Jefferson conceded that if invaded from the coast, Virginia could offer only feeble resistance. Surprisingly, Jefferson considered an attack on Virginia improbable, despite its vulnerability. British General Sir Henry Clinton, Jefferson believed, would be loathe to send the required men from New York, thus reducing his strength in that theater. If a flotilla was sent, the governor reasoned that the powerful French fleet could either defeat it or box it in. A third reason for Virginia's relative safety was, in Jefferson's estimation, that it lacked significant military targets. But the state had for four years supplied large numbers of men and great quantities of materiel to the effort for independence, the fact of which the British cabinet was well aware.

In late October of 1780, a British fleet arrived unexpectedly in the Chesapeake Bay. British Gen. Alexander Leslie and a few thousand troops were put ashore near Portsmouth and began fortifying. When, almost exactly a month later, Leslie and his men re-embarked for points farther south, Jefferson's views on Virginia's relative security seemed justified.

But with the arrival of 1781, dark war clouds again gathered over the Chesapeake. On January 5, a British force, under the despised traitor Benedict Arnold, sailed up the James River and took possession of Richmond, the state capital. The small contingent of Virginia militia tasked with interrupting his advance offered no resistance. Governor Jefferson, desperately riding his mount to exhaustion as he tried to organize a defense, observed the enemy from Manchester across the river. After destroying a foundry and precious military stores, Arnold's raiding force fell downriver to a fortified position at Portsmouth.

Soon after this time it was discovered that Gen. Charles Cornwallis, overall British commander of the southern department, was moving his sizable army north from North Carolina. From New York, Sir Henry Clinton began sending reinforcements to Virginia by sail. Monitoring these events from the north, American General-in-Chief George Washington realized that the British intended on seizing Virginia by main force. To bolster the militia defenders of the state of Virginia Washington dispatched one of his favorite officers, the youthful Marquis de Lafayette. Lafayette arrived in Richmond on April 29 with a corps of 800 northern veterans. He was just hours ahead of a British advance force.

On May 10, the Virginia Legislature determined to quit the state capital because of the rapidly deteriorating military situation. They decided to meet two weeks later in Charlottesville, but it was not until May 28 that a quorum was present. "Retiring before the enemy," penned Lee, "the government of the proud Commonwealth of Virginia not only lost all semblance of impressiveness. In the process of transferring its seat from Richmond to Charlottesville it practically dissolved."

Once arrived in the relative security of the Piedmont the first priority for the Virginia General Assembly became the defense of the Old Dominion. The scenario was grim. The British were suddenly present in huge force, the state capital had fallen, and the government was on the run. Many of the political and military leaders questioned the seeming inaction of the executive. "What ills spring from the timidity and impotence of rulers!" wrote Lee. "In them attachment to the common cause is vain and illusory, unless guided in times of difficulty by courage, wisdom, and concert." Jefferson had become the mere shadow of a governor.

Moving north to attack Lafayette, Cornwallis arrived in Petersburg on May 20 and began consolidating his powerful forces. The state was now the theater of the most active British operations. Lafayette faced 7,200 British regulars, many of whom had fought in the British victories of Guilford Court-House and Camden. Against this array Lafayette could muster only 3,100. "I am not strong enough," he wrote to his mentor Washington, "even to get beaten." Wisely, the Marquis decided not to risk combat. On May 27 he pulled his forces out of Richmond and marched toward Fredericksburg hoping to affect a junction with reinforcements coming from the north.

General Cornwallis occupied Richmond and pursued the American "rabble" as far as the North Anna River. Lafayette skillfully used his rearguard to keep the British at arm's length. Frustrated at not being able to catch the "aspiring boy," as he referred to Lafayette,

Lord Cornwallis determined to penetrate the interior of the state. He was well aware that his presence in Virginia had stirred a flurry of military activity. The revolutionary forces were standing off from his army, and around that periphery they were mustering their strength. Cornwallis heard that the Virginia legislature intended on putting out a call for eighteen-months' men for the Continental Line. At the urgent plea of the frantic governor, militias were also forming and military stores—what was left of them—were being concentrated.

From his position on the North Anna, Lord Cornwallis on June 3 unleashed two large raiding forces to slash into the heart of the state. "I therefore took advantage of the Marquis's passing the Rhappahannock [*sic*]" Cornwallis later wrote, "and detached Lieut. Cols. Simcoe and Tarleton to disturb the [Virginia General] Assembly then sitting at Charlottesville and to destroy the stores there, at Old Albemarle Court-House [Scottsville], and the Point of Fork. . . . " British officers Banastre Tarleton and John Graves Simcoe were well-known—and feared—as aggressive, independent commanders. Cornwallis marched southwest with the main body of British troops, crossing the South Anna River over Ground Squirrel Bridge. From there he continued westward to Thomas Jefferson's Elk Hill plantation on the James River. The Revolutionary War had finally come to central Virginia.

Lieut. Col. John Graves Simcoe advanced rapidly on June 3 against the Point of Fork Arsenal, located at the confluence of the Rivanna and James Rivers. Posted there was Baron von Steuben—the famous drillmaster of Valley Forge—in command of about 200 recruits for the Continental Army. Upon Simcoe's approach Steuben removed the stores and his troops to the south side of the James. When it appeared that Simcoe would cross, Steuben destroyed what he could not transport and retired farther south. Although Simcoe was relatively successful—he drove Stueben further away from the advancing Cornwallis—Lieut. Col. Banastre Tarleton's simultaneous raid on Charlottesville was an infinitely greater threat. In 1781 Tarleton's raid created no small amount of agitation and controversy. In the intervening years it has generated legends galore.

Lieut. Col. Banastre Tarleton had been born August 21, 1754, the son of a Liverpool merchant. He was of average height though heavily built, and had small, piercing black eyes. He began the war as a cornet of dragoons. The Revolution offered many opportunities for the use of cavalry and Tarleton rose quickly in rank. A mixed force of Loyalist cavalry and infantry was formed in Pennsylvania by Sir Henry Clinton in July of 1778. It was called the British Legion and Banastre Tarleton, just twenty-three years of age, became its commander with the rank of lieutenant colonel. The Legion adopted a uniform that included green jackets faced in white. Soon they were known as "Tarleton's Green Horse," and their leader as the "Green Dragoon."

In the southern campaign under Cornwallis Tarleton gained a reputation for being vigilant, rapid-moving, and often brutal. At Fishing Creek, North Carolina, on August 17, 1780, Tarleton with a detachment from the Legion fell upon a large camp of American militiamen. The unwary Americans were sleeping, cooking, and bathing. Tarleton's men rode into them sabers slashing. Those patriots not hacked to death scattered to the four winds. This action combined with others just as vicious won him the notice of the king. To the British, Banastre Tarleton, according to historian Winthrop Sargent, was "a capital horseman, the very model of a partisan leader."

Banastre Tarleton moved out on his raid in the early hours of June 3, 1781. His path of advance would take him between the North and South Anna Rivers—the distance was seventy miles. His force consisted of 180 dragoons from the British Legion and 17th Light Dragoons, augmented by seventy mounted infantrymen of the 23rd Regiment under a Captain Champagne. His orders directed him to Charlottesville, temporarily the capital of Virginia. The possible game on this hunt—the entire government of America's most populous state—included Patrick Henry, Richard Henry Lee, Benjamin Harrison, John Tyler, John Beckley, and Thomas Nelson Jr., all outspoken in Virginia's resistance to the authority of the crown. The route of advance also passed Monticello. We can only speculate on the plans Tarleton laid for Thomas Jefferson, author of the "seditious" Declaration of Independence.

The day was warm as the British troops rode westward. Tarleton rested his cavalrymen in the middle of the day, then pressed on into Louisa County. Riding four abreast, the 200-yard-long column encountered along its path closed doors and strangely silent barnyards. At 11 p.m. the "Green Dragoon" halted his men near Louisa Court-House for a three-hour respite "on a plentiful plantation." They had covered over half the distance to Charlottesville in less than a day. At 2 a.m. on June 4 Tarleton pushed on with every expectation of capturing the Virginia state government.

What Tarleton did not expect was the intervention of fate. In passing through Louisa the British raiders captured the attention of John "Jack" Jouett. Jouett was a strapping, twenty-seven-year-old captain of the Virginia militia. His father, John Sr., sold beef to the Continental Army and was proprietor of the Swan Tavern in Charlottesville where some of the Assemblymen were meeting. Jack Jr. was attending to some of his father's "business," as the accounts say, at the Cuckoo Tavern in Louisa when he saw the enemy raiders trot pass. Jouett instantly realized their objective. It was 10 o'clock, the night of June 3. Jouett mounted his thoroughbred and headed off towards Charlottesville, forty miles away. He was alone in his mission, but a brilliant full moon and his knowledge of the back roads would aid him.

Tarleton got an early start on June 4. Before dawn his men overtook twelve wagons laden with clothing for the Continental Army. The pitifully weak guard scattered at the British approach. "The waggons [sic] and stores were burnt," noted Tarleton, "that no time might be lost, or diminution of force made, by giving them an escort."

As the sun came up over the backs of the raiders, the ridgeline of the Southwest Mountains rose up ahead. Just after daybreak Tarleton made a side trip to Castle Hill, home of the famous Dr. Thomas Walker. Dr. Walker by 1781 had already made a huge contribution to the growth and prosperity of Albemarle County. He had explored the passes of the Appalachians (thus showing the way to Kentucky and beyond), helped established Charlottesville, negotiated with the native Indians, and represented the Piedmont to the House of Burgesses. The morning of June 4, however, was not a happy one for Walker. The household was startled awake by the hoofbeats that reverberated between the white clapboard house and the spur of the mountain. Green-jacketed dragoons filled the yard at Castle Hill, their accoutrements jangling as they dismounted. They forced the door and were quickly in the entranceway before Walker's visiting dignitaries could be rousted. "Some of the principal gentlemen of Virginia, who had fled to the borders of the mountains for security," wrote Tarleton, "were taken out of their beds."

A small British unit under Capt. David Kinloch was sent by Tarleton to nearby Belvoir, the home of Dr. Walker's son John. Here was enacted a scene more reminiscent of a civil war. Years earlier—according to historian Robert Bass Duncan—when the captain was preparing to leave England for America, the women of the family begged him not to kill his first cousin, Francis Kinloch. Francis was a member of Congress from South Carolina, an American patriot. "No I won't kill him," David reportedly told the ladies, "but I will be sure to take him prisoner!" Surely in making this statement Kinloch recognized the overwhelming odds against its realization. In the rising light of morning, Captain Kinloch and his party dismounted alongside Belvoir. But their arrival had awakened the occupants, Suddenly, a familiar-looking form—clad only in a nightshirt—fled from the rear of the dwelling. Captain Kinloch immediately gave chase on foot shouting "Wait, cousin Francis, you know I could always beat you in a race!"

Meanwhile, at Dr. Walker's Tarleton spent about half an hour watering and resting the horses and paroling some of his collected prisoners. Along with Francis Kinloch his men had captured William and Robert Nelson, brothers of General Thomas Nelson of Virginia. "Part [of the prisoners] were paroled, and left with their families," wrote Tarleton, "while others who were suspected to be more hostile in their sentiments, were carried off." Also taken was Judge Peter Lyons, who pleaded that because of poor health— he weighed 300 pounds—he should be left behind. Evidently Tarleton considered him "hostile," and ordered him to borrow a horse from Dr. Walker.

Legends have grown up like weeds around the truth of Tarleton's stopover at Walker's. They center on Walker's various attempts at delaying the expedition, thus saving Jefferson and the legislature from capture. One story has Dr. Walker making much to-do over measuring the height of Tarleton's orderly. Supposedly a notch carved into a hallway door frame—that still remains— measures in at six feet, nine inches. Another tale relates how the good doctor had an elaborate breakfast prepared for the enemy chief. Yet another has three separate meals prepared, the first two stolen by Tarleton's famished troopers. Meal or no, "the Green Dragoon" and his men were soon mounted and headed toward the gap in the Southwest Mountains—Pantops. The sun was well up and Charlottesville lay just beyond.

But Captain Jouett was not to be outdone by the British raiders. He had ridden all through the night, making the entire trip in just over six hours. While the British slept near Louisa Court-House he slipped around them to the south. (Perhaps later he noticed the light from the burning wagon train to the north.) Jouett used little-known roads and narrow, brush-covered cow paths when necessary. For the rest of his life he bore facial scars from his ride through the underbrush.

Jouett crossed the Rivanna below Monticello and wearily spurred his mount up the small mountain Jefferson called home. The time was approximately 4:30 a.m. The unexpected clatter from Jouett's mount brought one of the Monticello house servants to the door. Once his purpose was announced the entire household was alerted. Thomas Jefferson at the time was hosting a few members of both houses of the General Assembly. When the exhausted Captain Jouett remounted to carry the word into Charlottesville, Jefferson stepped out onto the east portico and handed him a fortifying glass of his best Madeira. Surprisingly the assemblymen were not panicked by the news. Perhaps the whole experience of the previous month had adapted them to the concept of "governing from the saddle." As Jefferson later wrote, the legislators "breakfasted at leisure," then packed and rode into Charlottesville.

Thomas Jefferson watched his fellow patriots depart then sent his family off by carriage to Col. Edward Carter's Blenheim, an estate some miles to the south. To everyone that morning he appeared calm and unhurried. Perhaps he believed it his duty. He was the captain of a rapidly sinking ship of state. He told his blacksmith to re-shoe his favorite mount. Then he busied himself with no small task—the organization and packing of his most important papers. This occupied his time for at least two hours. When the greater part of this was done, he decided to check on the progress of events. On Carter's Mountain, just above Monticello, Jefferson had set up a four-foot-long telescope. With it he scoured the nearby roads and Charlottesville for signs of the enemy.

The enemy were by then close indeed. As Tarleton's advance pounded through the gap in the Southwest Mountains, the rooftops of Charlottesville were plainly visible atop the next ridge to the west. The government of the state of Virginia must have seemed his for the taking. When the green-jacketed vanguard approached the Rivanna River below town, however, they reined in at the sight of armed men on the opposite side. Capt. John Martin of the Virginia Militia had been stationed at the ford with 200 men. They pulled off a few hurried shots but Tarleton's blood was up and he was eager to bag his game. He ordered an immediate attack. "The cavalry charged through the water with very little loss," Tarleton wrote proudly, "and routed the detachment posted at that place."

As soon as 100 of his men had splashed over the Rivanna, Tarleton ordered another swift advance. Within moments the dragoons thundered onto the streets of Charlottesville "to continue the confusion of the Americans," as noted Tarleton, "and to apprehend, if possible, the governor and the assembly." In these objectives, however, Tarleton was left largely unrewarded. Jefferson, he learned to his dismay, was not in town. Neither was the vast majority of the assemblymen. Forewarned by the ubiquitous Captain Jouett, most of the legislators had made good their escape. But not before they quickly convened, resolved to meet in three days at Staunton—beyond the safety of the Blue Ridge—then immediately adjourned. Perhaps, however, the adjournment was not quite quick enough. "Seven members of the assembly were secured," wrote Tarleton (although, unfortunately, he failed to name them), while "a Brig. General Scott, and several officers and men, were killed, wounded, or taken."

To nab Jefferson at Monticello, Tarleton detached a Captain McLeod and a party of dragoons. As the English ascended the little mountain they encountered no opposition. By this time, however, Jefferson had not only observed the enemy in Charlottesville but had been warned again. Capt. Christopher Hudson was on his way that day to join Lafayette's army. He was mistakenly told by a Mr. Long that Jefferson was unaware of the approaching enemy. Hudson later wrote that he galloped to Monticello "where I found Mr. Jefferson perfectly tranquill, & undisturbed. At the captain's "earnest request," however, Jefferson "left his house." Not ten minutes later, McLeod and his men broke through the trees into the clearing that surrounded the mountaintop villa.

At almost the last possible moment, Jefferson had sent for his mount. The blacksmith brought up the horse at a trot and Jefferson rode off to catch up with his family. The roads were unsafe, he reasoned, so he rode first up over Carter's Mountain. From the heights he looked back at Monticello in the agony that he would return only to a pile of ashes. He was leaving behind his home, his position as executive of the state, and perhaps what little dignity remained to him as a public figure. That evening he joined his family at Blenheim for what must have been a horribly gloomy dinner. "[T]he fates pursued Jefferson into the depths of the forest," wrote biographer Dumas Malone, "and the feeble government collapsed under the blows of the enemy."

When Captain McLeod confidently cantered up to the house he encountered only Martin Hemings, Jefferson's body servant. Moments earlier Martin had been lowering the household silver and other valuables through a trap door in the portico to Caesar, another slave. With the approach of the raiders Martin dropped the door leaving Caesar alone in the darkness with the booty. He remained there quietly for eighteen hours. Martin meanwhile escorted the enemy captain through the house, according to Henry S. Randall, with the dignity of "the seneschal of a surrendered medieval castle." Later in the day one of McLeod's dragoons put a pistol to Martin's chest and threatened to fire if he did not reveal the direction of Jefferson's flight. "Fire away then," replied the bondsman.

Luckily, Monticello was not destroyed by McLeod's men. "I did not suffer by Colonel Tarleton," Jefferson wrote in 1788. "On the contrary, he behaved very genteelly with me.... He gave strict orders to Captain McLeod to suffer nothing to be injured. . . . Captain McLeod preserved everything with sacred care."

Meanwhile Charlottesville swarmed with Tarleton's dragoons. As the excitement of the chase wore off they set about destroying military property. They burned a large quantity of stores they discovered in the neighborhood, and, noted Tarleton, "1000 new firelocks that had been manufactured at Fredericksburg were broken. Upwards of 400 barrels of powder were destroyed. Several hogsheads of tobacco, and some continental clothing and accoutrements, shared the same fate."

The government had scattered in all directions. "Such terror and confusion you have no idea of," wrote the daughter of Jacquelin Ambler, a member of Jefferson's council, "Governor, Council, everybody scampering." One of the delegates, Gen. Edward Stevens, recovering from a wound received at Guilford Court-House, made it away only because he was, according to historian Virginius Dabney "plainly dressed and mounted on a shabby horse."

A delegate that did not escape was Capt. Daniel Boone. Boone was a new member of the House of Delegates from one of the western counties that later became part of Kentucky. When the legislature skedaddled, Boone and several others stayed behind to help load wagons with public records. As the enemy cavalrymen entered Charlottesville, Boone and Jack Jouett, recalled Boone's son Nathan in 1851, "started off in a slow, unconcerned walk when they were overtaken, questioned hastily & dismissed." As Boone walked away Jouett yelled out "Wait a minute Capt. Boone & I'll go with you." A quick British officer asked, "Ah, is he a Captain?" and immediately ordered two of his men to take Boone into custody. Thanks to Jack Jouett, Daniel Boone spent the night of June 4 in a coalhouse near the British camp. The next morning he presented a filthy appearance when taken before Tarleton for interrogation. Boone explained his rank by referring to his commission in Lord Dunmore's pre-Revolutionary War army. Tarleton released him.

Banastre Tarleton remained in Charlottesville for one day, until June 5. The raider established his headquarters at The Farm, a huge estate owned by Col. Nicholas Meriwether Lewis. The Farm was just downhill from town, along the banks of the Rivanna within sight of Monticello. Lewis had married Dr. Walker's eldest daughter Molly. The home stood midway between Charlottesville

and the river. Family tradition holds that while Mrs. Lewis watched, Tarleton and his men rode up to the house directly through her rose gardens and shrubbery. Perhaps to appease the mistress of the property Tarleton exclaimed, "What a paradise!" The feisty Molly supposedly fired back, "Then why do you disturb it!?"

Tarleton and his horsemen departed Charlottesville the next day. He proceeded down the Rivanna River and linked up with the other British raiders after Simcoe's force had destroyed the Point of Fork Arsenal. Together the raiding forces made the short march down the James to Cornwallis encamped at Elk Hill. Lewis family legend has Tarleton's men riding off with the entire flock of Molly's prize ducks, minus the drake. Perturbed by the Britisher's thoughtlessness, Mrs. Lewis had the drake delivered to Tarleton by a swiftly mounted servant. Tarleton sent the bondsman back to Mrs. Lewis with his "profoundest thanks." The ordeal was over for Charlottesville, but not for Thomas Jefferson.

Jefferson's opponents from the state of Virginia and beyond played up his ineptitude as a war-time governor as well as his "cowardly" retreat from the raiders. By this treatment Thomas Jefferson was deeply wounded. Even years later the Federalists tried to make light of what they called the "Affair of Carter's Mountain." Jefferson's mood for the rest of 1781 is best described in his own words. After Cornwallis had surrendered he penned his excuse to Washington for not visiting the general on such a momentous occasion. He would have journeyed to Washington's side, wrote Jefferson, but for "the state of perpetual decrepitude to which I am unfortunately reduced." Thomas Jefferson at the time was thirty-eight, but the last six months of his term as governor had made him feel prematurely old, decrepit, and defeated.

All that remains on Mulberry Row of the Joinery.
(Photo by the author.)

III

"A Most Unpleasant Contrast"

Slavery Along Mulberry Row

"My opinion has ever been that, until more can be done for them, we should endeavor, with those whom fortune has thrown on our hands, to feed and clothe them well, protect them from ill usage, require such reasonable labor only as is performed voluntarily by freemen, and be led by no repugnancies to abdicate them, and our duties to them."
                                                                — *Thomas Jefferson, 1814*

It was a wonderfully bracing morning in the second week of November, 1824. The Piedmont's Indian summer, with its temperate breezes, had just recently given way to autumn's invigorating nip. Along a roundabout that girded Monticello Mountain jostled a jet-black landau. Inside the open coach the passengers—two distinguished older gentlemen and a man in his mid-forties—fixed their gaze westward through an aperture in the trees. Twenty-five miles distant, lifted above a snow-white ocean of fog, the ancient range of mountains was cloaked in majestic blue. In the immediate foreground, alongside the rutted path, however, the rising sunlight revealed dazzling shades of yellow, orange, and red. Overhead a noisy wing of Canada geese stretched their long, black necks to the south.

Driving the carriage was Israel Gillett Jefferson, a twenty-four-year-old slave. His riders had, for the most part, remained quiet—caught up in the breathtaking view. But when the vista was shut off they picked up a conversation that the bondsman found particularly interesting. He perked up his ears.

"[T]he slaves ought to be free . . ." remarked the Marquis de Lafayette to his old friend—as Israel recounted forty-nine years later for an Ohio newspaperman. Lafayette said that "he gave his best services to and spent his money in behalf of the Americans freely because he felt that they were fighting for a great and noble principle—the freedom of mankind." The vehicle rumbled across a rough spot as the venerable revolutionary drove home the point. Now, "instead of all being free," Lafayette continued passionately, "a portion were [still] held in bondage." And, Israel recalled, the "Sage of Monticello" listened pensively while the Frenchman emphasized that "it would be mutually beneficial to masters and slaves if the latter were educated. . . ."

"Mr. Jefferson," remembered the carriage man, "replied that he thought the time would come when the slaves would be free, but did not indicate when or in what manner they would get their freedom. He seemed to think that the time had not then arrived." With the sun well up the landau wheeled along the well-packed earth of the mountain's upper roundabout. Three slaves hailed the driver as the vehicle passed the sawpit. Fifty feet beyond two young black boys carrying a weighty bundle of nailrod stepped aside as the clattering horses approached. From inside the nailery could be heard the metal din of over a dozen hammers. Mulberry Row's busy day had already begun.

Visitors to Monticello during Jefferson's retirement were literally surrounded by the evidence of his wide-ranging intellect: the mansion itself, an intimate look into his architectural genius; his Entrance Hall with its eclectic assortment of Old World art and Native American objects; his paintings of American explorers; the fossilized bones of the American *Mastodon*; the winding garden-walk, etc. Monticello—and its fabulous Jefferson collection—is still available for study because the mansion itself was built with permanence in mind. "A country whose buildings are of wood," Jefferson wrote, "can never increase in its improvements to any considerable degree." By contrast, next to nothing remains to tell the story of most of the people who lived on the top of the "little mountain" itself—the African American slaves. Their homes, and most of the structures in which they labored, were built of wood.

Although Monticello, the plantation, was subdivided into four farms—Tufton, Lego, Shadwell, and Pantops—as many as one-third of Jefferson's Albemarle County slaves worked, and were quartered, along Mulberry Row, just a few paces east of the villa. These slaves, as many as forty at any one given time, labored tirelessly toward the domestic happiness of the Jefferson and Randolph families, and the prosperity of the plantation community. They were house servants and errand runners, weavers, carriage men and stable hands, chefs and cooks, washerwomen, sawyers, tinsmiths, blacksmiths and nail-makers, gardeners, carpenters, furniture-builders, and masons. Their way of life, the buildings in which they lived and loved, and the artifacts of their existence have passed into the obscuring mist of history.

Mulberry Row was named for the berry-laden trees that lined its 1,000-foot-long stretch. Jefferson's original plan was to construct on the path a long, 400-foot building that would house iron and woodworking operations as well as a slaughterhouse and storage rooms for domestic necessities. This scheme, like so many of his others, however, never saw the light of day. Mulberry Row instead became the site of a number of temporary structures designed to service the mansion and the 5,000-acre plantation.

In 1796 Mulberry Row was the site of seventeen buildings. Jefferson's Insurance Plat (or map) of that year locates them along the lane and lists their dimensions and composition. They included, running north to south: a 105-foot-long one-story stable made of wood; three small, log "servant's houses" measuring twelve by fourteen feet each, "with wooden chimneys, & earth floors"; a slightly bigger slave cabin with an attached shed, which, ironically, was larger and included a brick floor; a one-story "stone outhouse" known as the "weaver's cottage"; another servant's house, this one measuring twenty by twelve feet; and a wash house.

Seven of the next eight structures represented much of the industrial nature of activities on Mulberry Row. These included: a forty-three by sixteen foot smokehouse/dairy; a small storehouse for nailrod; "a necessary house"; a thirty-seven by eighteen foot "smith and nailer's shop" with an attached fifty-foot-long nailery; a fifty-seven by eighteen foot "joiner's shop" (of which the stone chimney remains); a nearby storehouse for "planks & such things"; a sawpit; and two small coal sheds. To complete the picture a ten-foot-high paling fence skirted the entire length of Mulberry Row—"either touching or passing very near to every house"—and surrounded the two-acre vegetable garden and the 400-tree orchard that lay just below.

With but this quick description it's easy to visualize Mulberry Row as the epicenter of activity at Monticello. House servants scurried back and forth across the portion of the path nearest the mansion while the southern length was filled with enslaved tradesmen, their tools, and mule carts hauling raw materials. (Additionally, Monticello's southeastern terrace—which runs parallel to Mulberry Row—featured a large kitchen, and slave quarters for perhaps two more African American families.) These bondsmen—men and women—toiled in the shadow of opulence. "We passed the outhouses for the slaves and workmen," wrote Margaret Bayard Smith after a visit in 1809: "They are all much better than I have seen on any other plantation, but to an eye unaccustomed to such sights, they appear poor and their cabins form a most unpleasant contrast with the palace that rises so near them."

The average workday ran from dawn until dusk—a schedule that meant fourteen-hour days during high summer, and nine-hour days in winter. In return Jefferson's slaves received food, a twice-yearly issuance of clothing, and housing along Mulberry Row—where sometimes a family of three generations, perhaps as many as ten individuals, were assigned to one log cabin. Monticello's weekly food ration, for adults, consisted of a peck of meal and a pound of pork, augmented by salted herring and molasses. Milk and vegetables were added during the summer months. Sunday was their day of rest. The Sabbath was "a great blessing to the world," wrote Jefferson to Benjamin Rush, "more especially to poor people and slaves." Jefferson's slaves were also given four days around Christmas, plus a few other holidays.

Slave children on Mulberry Row, and the plantation at large, were free to play until their seventh birthday. From that age "till 10 years old [they] serve as nurses," wrote Jefferson in his Farm Book; "from 10 to 16 the boys make nails [and] the girls spin; at 16 [they either] go into the ground [become field-hands] or learn trades." And there were trades aplenty. "[T]o be independent for the comforts of life," wrote the master of Monticello, "we must fabricate them ourselves. We must place the manufacturer by the side of the agriculturist. . . ." Hired white artisans such as blacksmiths, carpenters and masons took on selected African Americans as apprentices. These, in turn, trained their fellow bondsmen. For those workers along Mulberry Row, Jefferson oftentimes provided detailed instructions. "[Jefferson] had many very respectable workmen among his slaves, whose expertness had been greatly improved," wrote University of Virginia Professor George Tucker, "both by his instructions and the diversified occupation which he afforded them. The carriage in which he ordinarily rode, his garden seats, even some of his household furniture, were the joint work of himself and his slaves."

Some of Jefferson's "household furniture"—such as the large seed press in the Book Room, and one of the campeachy chairs which grace the parlor—was created at the joinery by the slave joiner John Hemings (1776–c.1830). John was the son of Betty Hemings, whom Jefferson inherited from his father-in-law, and half-brother to the now world-renowned Sally. He began his working life as an "out-carpenter," helping to erect slave buildings along Mulberry Row, then quickly advanced into the trades of wheelwright and furniture-maker. "He was a first-rate workman—a very extra workman," remembered overseer Edmund Bacon: "He could make anything that was wanted in woodwork. He learned his trade of [James]

Dinsmore [a white joiner who fashioned most of Monticello's interior fittings]. [Hemings] made most of the woodwork of Mr. Jefferson's fine carriage."

In the stone "weaver's cottage" older slave women and young slave girls worked at Hargreaves spinning jennies, producing wool, hemp and cotton cloth for slave clothing. "[Jefferson] got his cotton from Richmond in bateaux," recalled Edmund Bacon in 1861. "He had in his factory three spinning machines. One had thirty-six spindles, one eighteen, and one six. The hands used to learn on the little one." Betty Hemings's daughter Nance (1761–c.1827) labored in this "factory" outbuilding during the American Revolution under the tutelage of resident white weaver Bartholomew Kindred. Jefferson's Farm Book records that Harriet Hemings, daughter of Sally, was working as a weaver in 1801 at the age of fourteen.

The log smokehouse/dairy was added to Mulberry Row in 1790. In this building meat was stored and cured, either by smoking or pickling. This operation was particularly important as pork and bacon were solid staples of the slave diet. In the dairy, milking was done in the summer months and, occasionally, butter was churned (although this condiment was normally purchased). As this facility was so integral to the maintenance of the plantation, it is fascinating to consider the fact that it was overseen, for a while, by Ursula, an African American slave. Ursula was a trusted house servant who had been purchased by Jefferson at the insistence of his wife. Some of Ursula's other skills included the baking of pastry and the bottling of cider, one of the "Sage of Monticello's" favorite beverages.

Ursula's husband, Great George, and one of their sons, Isaac Jefferson, were both employed in the "smith and nailer's shop." The blacksmith shop was constructed in 1793: the nailery was attached to it but a few years later. Monticello's slave smiths shoed horses, produced the metal fittings for the vehicles he designed and repaired the vast number of farming implements used on the plantation. Significant work, indeed, but Jefferson focused much of his attention on the "factory" that sat alongside. "Of this nail manufactory [he] was inordinately proud," wrote historian John Chester Miller: "he described himself as a nail maker as well as a farmer, the only virtuous occupation besides farming that he was willing to admit to his pantheon."

"Mr. Jefferson had a nail factory a good many years, which was a great convenience to the people and very profitable," Edmund Bacon recollected. "He worked ten hands in it, had two fires, and five hands at a fire." The raw material was nailrod—long, thin strips of square metal shipped down from Philadelphia to Milton on the Rivanna River. The rods, which varied according to the desired nail-size, came in bundles—some measuring ten feet long and weighing close to 50 pounds. When Jefferson was at home he would often visit the nailery early, in order to carefully weigh, and dole out, the metal rods. Isaac Jefferson said in 1847 that he "carred [sic] on the nail business at Monticello seven years—made money at that. Mr. Jefferson had the first [nail] cutting machine 'twas said, that ever was in Vaginny [sic]—sent over from England. Made wrought nails and cut nails, to shingle and lath." On an average day in 1796, between 5,000 and 10,000 nails were cut and hammered into seven different sizes.

To the young slave nailers that were the most efficient—that is, produced the most nails with the least amount of wastage—Jefferson often presented bonuses. "[He] give [sic] them that wukked [sic] the best a suit of red or blue; encouraged them mightily," remembered Isaac: "Isaac calls him a mighty good master." Some of the youngsters also earned a few coins. "These hands could clear two dollars a day, besides paying for the coal and iron rods," said Bacon. "We supplied the stores all over the country with nails and sold a great many to the people to build their houses. I sold Mr. [James] Monroe the nails to build his house."

But "factory" laborers were not the only enslaved individuals who walked the hard-packed earth of Mulberry Row. Peter Hemings (1770–c.1830) was a house servant who was later instructed in the mysteries of French cuisine by his older brother James (who had traveled to Paris with Jefferson). He was, evidently, very skilled at baking. "Pray enable yourself to direct us here how to make muffins in Peter's method," Jefferson wrote to daughter Martha after being disappointed by the best efforts of the chef at the President's House. Wormley Hughes (1781–1858) toiled in the nailery as a teenager but also performed tasks in the mansion. Hughes was later trained as a gardener by Scotsman Robert Bailey and, according to one of Jefferson's granddaughters, "armed with spade and hoe," helped his master lay out the beautifully designed flower beds. Wormley Hughes dug Jefferson's grave in 1826.

Sally Hemings (1773–1835) was the daughter of Betty Hemings and, allegedly, Thomas Jefferson's father-in-law John Wayles. (If this part of the story is true, Sally was half-sister to her master's wife, Martha.) As a child she probably served as a "nurse" to Jefferson's youngest daughter Maria, nicknamed Polly. When fourteen years old Sally Hemings traveled with Maria across the Atlantic to France and remained there—as Maria's attendant—throughout the balance of Jefferson's term as ambassador. After his return to Monticello in 1789 Sally worked as a house servant and lady's maid. In 1802 a Richmond newspaper printed the allegation that Jefferson had taken Sally Hemings as his mistress, while in France, and had already fathered several slave children by her. One of her sons, Madison Hemings, told an Ohio newspaperman in 1873 that Jefferson was his father, and that his mother Sally had told him so. (The 1998 DNA study indicated a very strong possibility that Thomas Jefferson was, indeed, the father of Sally's youngest son Eston. This study, and the others that are sure to follow, will, no doubt, increase the interest in African American history at Monticello and help redefine Jefferson's personal life.)

The landau carrying Jefferson, the Marquis de Lafayette, and the Lafayette's son George rumbled down Mulberry Row toward the stable. Israel listened closely as his master spoke to the matter of educating slaves. "He was in favor of teaching the slaves to learn to read print," remembered the carriage man, "[but] to teach them to write would enable them to forge papers [and] they could no longer be kept in subjugation."

"This conversation was very gratifying to me," Israel later recalled, "and I treasured it up in my heart."

A Monticello vineyard in winter.
(Photo by the author.)

IV

FILIPPO MAZZEI:

Italian Genius, American Patriot

"An intimacy of forty years had proved to me [Mazzei's] great worth; and a friendship, which had begun in personal acquaintance, was maintained after separation, without abatement by a constant interchange of letters. His esteem too in this country was very general; his early and zealous cooperation in the establishment of our independence having acquired for him here a great degree of favor."
- Thomas Jefferson to Giovanni Carmignani, July 18, 1816

W hile the brigantine *Johnston* gently rolled in her berth at Hob's Hole, Virginia—on the Rappahannock River— one of her passengers, a distinguished Italian gentleman, furiously penned a letter in English. The forty-nine-year-old native of Tuscany was small, wiry, and graying, but through his large intense eyes shone a unique brilliance, and a level of energy befitting a much younger man. In the dim light, and relative security, of his cramped stateroom he itemized his growing anxiety. The mission was already in terrible jeopardy, he feared, as was the safety of his official documents. It was the evening of June 13, 1779—during the fifth year of the American struggle for independence.

"I have put my papers with a 4 pounds [*sic*] ball in a bag to be thrown overboard, if prudence should require it," he wrote future president James Madison, "but I have first made an extract, and have interlined it in old papers of private accounts etc., which I don't think would be taken from me. . . . In case I should sink the papers and escape, the said memorandum will enable me to act while I am awaiting for the copies of my Commission and Instructions, the sending of which I hope you will not neglect."

But if he prayed that his apprehension would, perhaps, disperse with the drying of his ink, he prayed in vain. In a follow-up letter written from Urbanna—five days later, and twenty-seven miles downstream—the learned Italian further described his "disturbed mind." "[W]e have no more than 2 Americans on board," he penned, feeling outnumbered, "one of which is the cabbin-boy [sic]." And Capt. Andrew Paton, he wrote suspiciously, "has obliged me to put on board a prodigious quantity of provisions, besides other very costly conveniences. . . ." He also dreaded that Paton—whom he described as a Scotchman with an dislikable "physiognomy"—was a traitor to the American cause, colluding with the enemy.

Unfortunately, his fears were well-founded. On the morning of June 20, when the two-masted *Johnston* was thirty miles off the Virginia Capes, she was quickly overtaken by an English privateer. Into the sea fell the Tuscan's sack of important papers, and thus fell into British hands Filippo Mazzei: merchant, physician, horticulturist, vintner, Albemarle County resident—and special agent for the State of Virginia.

Filippo Mazzei (pronounced Mat-ZAY) was born at Poggio a Caiano, Tuscany, on December 25, 1730. He studied medicine, receiving a degree in surgery, and worked as a physician for a few years in Firenze (Florence) and Livorno (Leghorn) before taking his practice to Smyrna, Turkey, in 1752. But Filippo Mazzei was a man of much energy, and enthusiasm for life—he could not be held down by simply one profession. (Historian Dumas Malone, in fact, compared him to sixteenth-century Italian sculptor Benvenuto Cellini, a man often described as colorful and vigorous.) Mazzei soon decided that commerce, rather than surgery, was his real calling.

"So, encouraged by friends, in 1756 he moved to London, where he organized the firm of Martini and Company, importers of [Italian] cheese, wine and olive oil," wrote biographer Sister Margherita Marchione. "In London he made the acquaintance of Thomas Adams [a Virginia-born businessman] and Benjamin Franklin," she continued, "who urged him to come to America to introduce southern European cultures. Before he sailed for Virginia in 1773, he went back to his native Tuscany for the Grand Duke's permission to export the necessary materials and men." Mazzei brought to the Old Dominion "various agricultural implements and cuttings from vines, trees, and plants," she wrote. "He was also able to induce some peasants and a tailor to accompany him."

Mazzei's ship set sail from Livorno, Italy on September 2, 1773 and arrived in Williamsburg, Virginia's capital, two months later. A subsequent edition of the *Virginia Gazette* recorded that "The *Triumph* . . . from Leghorn [recently] arrived in [the] James River; in the latter, we hear, many gentleman came [as] passengers, in order to settle and cultivate vines in this colony." Indeed, thanks to the efforts of Thomas Adams, the Virginia legislature had promised Mazzei 5,000 acres in Augusta County, for the express purpose of establishing vineyards. ("I did not find it convenient to accept the grant," Mazzei later wrote in his autobiography entitled *My Life and Wanderings*, "because it consisted of many parcels far removed one from the other.")

Upon arriving in Virginia Mazzei and his laborers passed a brief period at the home of Francis Eppes, Thomas Jefferson's brother-in-law. Soon thereafter—in late November, 1773—Mazzei set out for the Shenandoah Valley together with Adams, whom the Tuscan called "my mentor." "[Adams] wished to see where it would be best to have his house built," wrote Mazzei, "and I, to find whether I could buy some land near him if I liked the location." "It was unfortunate for these plans," wrote Malone, "that they stopped for an evening at Monticello."

The next morning, as was his custom, the thirty-year-old Thomas Jefferson arose early. Perhaps he was surprised to find Mazzei also up and about. Excited about hosting a European visitor, Jefferson took him on one of his long rambles and showed off the advantages of the neighborhood. When the two, already fast friends, returned from their excursion, Adams, glancing at Jefferson said: "I see it on your face that you've taken him away from me; why, I expected as much."

It had all been decided in a twinkling. The land on the southeastern slopes of Monticello Mountain seemed perfect for Mazzei's vines, and some of it could be acquired from a poor farmer. Plus, as Jefferson's property was adjacent "and he had much more than he needed," remembered Mazzei, "he made me a gift of a tract of 2,000 acres." Within a short time a dozen other Italians arrived, "and to their delight the tall, friendly Virginian," wrote Malone, "talked with them in Tuscan, which he had picked up unaided."

Thus was introduced into Albemarle County Italian wine and vegetables, along with the distinctive tools the laborers had brought for their cultivation—spades and billhooks in particular—and their unique, short game jacket or hunting coat. Thus, too, was begun a friendship that would endure forty-three years.

"It's easy to understand what made Mazzei so appealing to Jefferson," wrote Hunter College professor Charles Guzzetta. "Thirteen years Jefferson's senior, Mazzei was well-educated and widely-traveled, an urbane and endlessly interesting sophisticate whose accomplishments and secure social position nevertheless did not stop him from leaving a well-established business to try his hand in the Virginia countryside. . . . In addition, Mazzei was Italian, and Jefferson was intrigued by Italian culture."

Filippo Mazzei named his new-found property "Colle," from the poetic Italian for hillock. Work on the acreage began immediately. "I started my men to clear the land," wrote the Tuscan, "beginning from the part under cultivation and continuing up beyond the hill on which I wished to situate my house. To speed up the work I hired two hard-working blacks. . . ." The hilltop that he was to call home was also cleared, leaving, he wrote, "some of the prettier trees here and there on the slope, pruning them so as to offer a beautiful sight."

Albemarle's newest immigrants were quite an interesting lot. Signor Giovanni Fabbroni, only fifteen years old, was described by

Mazzei as "an educated young Tuscan" with an amazing "fund of acquired knowledge." Another—Mazzei's "Piedmontese tailor"— was soon kept quite busy by the local demand for his talent. Filippo Mazzei's entourage also included his London partner's widow, Maria Martin, whom he married in 1774, and her daughter. And Antonio—or Anthony, as Mazzei called him—Giannini, a worker from Fibbialla whose descendants still reside in Central Virginia. Six more vignerons, young Luccans, arrived in Albemarle shortly thereafter, in early 1774, along with Carlo Bellini, who Jefferson later recommended to the post of professor of modern languages at the College of William and Mary.

During the winter of 1773–74 Filippo Mazzei, his first name now Americanized to "Philip," put his tremendous energy behind the enterprise at Colle. He announced what he called a "Proposal for forming a Company or Partnership, for the Purpose of raising and making Wine, Oil, agruminous Plants, and Silk," and had little difficulty enlisting subscribers. "Thirty-one prominent colonial leaders (including Lord Dunmore, George Washington, Thomas Jefferson)," wrote Marchione, "subscribed paying 50 pounds sterling per share. Virginians were eager to participate in his schemes for producing new products and for encouraging viniculture." "I am of the opinion," Mazzei later penned, "that when [Virginia] is populated in proportion to its area, the best wines in the world will be made there." But, despite his predictions—and much hard work—the "Wine Company" failed.

"The future," as noted Johann Wolfgang von Goethe, "casts its shadow before." At Colle all the workers were experienced Italian winegrowers. They knew what they were doing and they surmised quickly that the vines were not growing properly. Surprisingly, May of 1774 brought a frost unlike anything the longtime residents had ever seen. "The clusters of grapes, already big," wrote Mazzei, "froze along with the grain crops." Naturally the Tuscan sent to Italy for more vines. They were probably damaged in transit. So, in 1774 they planted again. In the spring of 1775 the vines pushed out shoots but

they still did not produce. In fact—following the general rule in use at the time—Mazzei's workers must certainly have cut them back. Colle's vines, therfore, would not have produced until 1776.

Perhaps it was all just as well. For by 1776 Mazzei's attention had long since been diverted to another, more interesting, matter. What could have possibly been more interesting? Politics—the emerging conflict with England.

"Mazzei early evinced an intense interest in the political life of the Colonies," wrote Richard Cecil Garlick, Jr., "especially in that of Virginia." During his many visits to Williamsburg he had been cordially received by George Washington, George Wythe, Richard Bland, George Mason, Peyton Randolph, and many other prominent individuals. In 1774 he had been introduced, in the capital, to Lord Dunmore and his wife—and by the governor was made a naturalized citizen of the Old Dominion. "Thinking perhaps that [Dunmore] could make a proselyte of me," penned Mazzei, "he unbosomed himself to me in such a way that I was able to see clearly the weakness of his mind and the meanness of his heart. . . . I informed Jefferson of what I had learned from the Governor, adding my opinion as to probable future developments."

The two soon decided to publish—through the gazettes—a periodic sheet of patriotic sentiments, "aiming," wrote the Tuscan, "to show the people how things really stood and how necessary it was to be prepared," in case of attack. "At first Mazzei wrote in Italian and Jefferson translated," wrote Garlick, "but after a while Jefferson persuaded him that his English was sufficiently good to stand even without revision." This series of newspaper articles, written under the pseudonym "Furioso"—it is interesting to note—appeared in the *Virginia Gazette* in 1774–75, the first few of which just prior to Jefferson's powerful *A Summary View of the Rights of British America* (printed the summer of 1774), and well before Thomas Paine's pamphlet *Common Sense* (which hit the streets in January of 1776).

Furthermore, one of the above-mentioned pieces contained the following sentences by Mazzei, in Italian, before transcription: *Tutti gli uomini sono per natura equalmente liberi e indipendenti. Questi eguaglianza é necessaria per costituire un governo libero.* (Which translates to: "All men are by nature equally free and independent. This equality is necessary in order to constitute a free government.") And, according to Marchione, "Jefferson's original draft of the Declaration of Independence contained the phrase 'and independent' ('that all men are created equal and independent. . . .')."

Mazzei later claimed that this collaborative effort caused the formation of the "Independent Companies" of volunteer militiamen in each county, and, wrote Garlick, "caused the election, later, of representatives to compose a 'Convention' instead of the Assembly." But the power of Mazzei's mind was also felt in areas outside the press. After only six months in Albemarle County the Tuscan was elected to the vestry and began spreading Jefferson's ideas on religious freedom through the church. Also, during the summer of 1774, Mazzei was elected to the county's twelve-man Committee of Correspondence.

With the threat of war scowling from the cannon-muzzles of English warships in the Chesapeake, the energetic Tuscan decided to involve himself even further. "When the British first landed troops at Hampton," Virginia in April of 1775, wrote Garlick, "Mazzei, Bellini and Jefferson joined the 'Independent Company' of Albemarle as privates." "The men wanted Jefferson to be an officer," remembered Mazzei, "but he was engaged in something of greater importance, being a member of the Convention. They wanted to make me a lieutenant, but I begged off as being unfit." For the expedition Mazzei took along three of his horses, sharing rides with other volunteers and enjoyed the nights spent out in the open.

As the company tramped toward the coast their numbers steadily grew. In Orange County they were joined by the Madison brothers, James and Ambrose. After covering eighty miles the volunteers were apprised by Patrick Henry that the British, hearing that armed men from all over Virginia were coming to face them, had, according to Mazzei, "thought it proper to reembark and leave." The plucky sons of Albemarle—including the two "adopted"—decided to disband and return home.

By 1776, the Tuscan horticulturist was an ever-present voice in central Virginia politics. His forty-page *Instructions of the Freeholders of Albemarle County to their Delegates in Convention*, written in May of 1776, was, wrote Marchione, "a concrete example of his desire to participate in the drafting of the constitution of the new state." In it he writes, for example, of "men now labouring under the oppression of Tyranny in other Countries who will fly to this free land." Julian Boyd, one of the editors of *The Papers of Thomas Jefferson* acknowledged in 1952 that Jefferson's own 1783 draft-constitution for Virginia was greatly influenced by Mazzei's political document.

By 1778, the revolutionary leaders of the Old Dominion were considering sending the Tuscan to Europe to further encourage immigration. Late that year, wrote Garlick, "[i]t was decided by Thomas Jefferson, Patrick Henry, George Mason, John Page and others, that Mazzei would be put to better use if he were sent over for the purpose of borrowing money from his friend, the Grand-Duke of Tuscany, for the State of Virginia."

It does not take too close a read between the lines here to sense that those in power were anxious to have Mazzei depart. Even at age forty-eight he still had the tendency to be exceedingly talkative, and overly assertive. Thomas Jefferson once admitted that Mazzei wore him out. And in a later missive to James Madison, Jefferson wrote that Mazzei's presence was sometimes worse "than a return of my double quotidian [or twice-daily] headache." In a letter to then-Virginia Delegate Thomas Adams dated January 27, 1779 Mazzei confided: "I am going to Europe in the service of our State."

Unfortunately, his mission was a failure. As noted above the Tuscan was captured off the Virginia Capes—along with his family, who were also onboard—and kept in confinement for a few months on British-held Long Island. When he finally arrived in Europe his fund-raising efforts were unsuccessful. Nonetheless, being paid six hundred luigi a year by Virginia, Mazzei remained and forwarded information to Jefferson, who was by then the state's governor.

Filippo Mazzei returned to Virginia, to "Colle," in 1783 but stayed on for only two years. "Still active politically," wrote Guzzetta, "he helped organize the Constitutional Society, an association for political discussion which included in its membership Madison, Monroe, Henry, and John Marshall."

The fifty-five-year-old Tuscan left Virginia for the last time in 1785. Still retaining much of his earlier energy and drive Mazzei's remaining years were no less eventful. In Paris he wrote his massive four-volume history of the colonies, *Recherches Historiques et Politiques sur les États-Unis de l'Amérique Septentrionale*—published in 1788—relying heavily on his Virginia contacts for details and information. During the same time he was employed by King Stanislaus of Poland as an agent, in Paris—and later moved to Warsaw as the sovereign's personal advisor. By 1792 he was living in Pisa on a pension granted him by the Czar of Russia.

Through it all he kept up a correspondence, and a warm relationship, with the "Sage of Monticello." (Oddly enough, Mazzei's wife—who had remained at "Colle"—had died in 1788 and was buried in the Jefferson-family cemetery.) Thomas Jefferson employed Mazzei's talents, and taste, in acquiring for America bits and pieces of the Italian culture. The Tuscan shipped to Jefferson Florentine portraits of Amerigo Vespucci and Columbus, sent him various seeds and plants, and—when the Virginian was president—hired for him Italian sculptors needed for the work on the new federal capitol.

Filippo Mazzei died in 1816, three years after completing his endlessly entertaining memoirs. Jefferson, on learning of his friend's death wrote: "He had some peculiarities (and who of us has not?), but he was of solid worth; honest, able, zealous in sound principles, moral and political, constant in friendship, and punctual in all his undertakings." He had gained renown as an agriculturist, vintner, and political activist. Mazzei was particularly proud of his service to his adopted state—Virginia. His life had been filled to overflowing with much complexity—stirring events and dazzling personalities. In the end, in his memoirs, however, Filippo Mazzei reflected on life's simplicities. "Beyond bringing about the happiness [of my friends]," he wrote, "I do not think I have done anything but be a gardener."

Thomas Jefferson in Paris.

V

"The Tranquil Pursuits of Science":

Thomas Jefferson & Science

The trip to Philadelphia took ten days. Departing from Monticello on February 20, 1797, the fifty-three-year-old Thomas Jefferson journeyed northeastward through Orange and Spotsylvania Counties. Thanks to the frigid season, it was a "tremendous undertaking," as he called it—the byways, though well-traveled and well-marked, were deeply rutted and brick-hard. They rattled his carriage and quickly tired his steeds. In Dumfries, Virginia, therefore—in order to spare his horses from the great effort—Jefferson sent his personal vehicle back home and boarded a public stage.

Coming out of retirement—he had resigned from George Washington's cabinet over three years earlier—Thomas Jefferson was simultaneously embarking on a very different "public stage." In Alexandria, during a brief stopover, he received the official notification—a certificate—of his election to the post of vice president of the United States. He had learned of the results earlier, naturally, and had written to Dr. Benjamin Rush "[a] more tranquil and unoffending station could not have been found for me." Jefferson had at first hesitated to travel to Philadelphia, the nation's capital, simply to take the oath of office that could be administered anywhere. But he quickly changed his mind out of respect to the public and especially to dispel the rumor that he deemed the second office beneath his acceptance.

Attending the inaugural ceremony was not his only purpose for traveling to Philadelphia, however, for safely packed away in his luggage were several fossilized bones of a massive animal that had been recently dug out of a cave in Greenbrier County, Virginia. He thought the creature—which he called *Megalonyx* or "Great Claw"—was unknown to science and he was eager, while in the city, to present his paper regarding the discovery to the American Philosophical Society, the country's foremost scientific organization. More importantly, the members of the Society were just as eager to install him as their new president. Thus the illustrious institution founded by Benjamin Franklin in 1743—the year, coincidently, of Jefferson's birth—would soon be headed by Thomas Jefferson, "by whose genius and knowledge," the Society had written him, "our national name will preserve a distinguished place in the annals of science." The ceremony was to take place the evening before he became vice president. "It was as high an honour" [sic], according to Jefferson eulogizer Samuel L. Mitchill, "as can be conferred upon a scientific man in our country."

In Philadelphia, therefore—over the course of two days—Thomas Jefferson would assume two incredibly important positions: the nation's second-highest in politics, and its first in science. There's no question as to which of the two he found the most interesting.

Thomas Jefferson was forever torn between the call to public service and his deep longing for a private life devoted to his family and his amazingly eclectic range of interests. Of these, science was perhaps his greatest passion. "Nature intended me for the tranquil pursuits of science," he wrote Du Pont de Nemours in 1809, "by rendering them my supreme delight." Only the "enormities of the times," he continued, had forced him to focus instead on the "boisterous ocean of political passions." Yet, for someone who labored so long as a public servant—he spent, after all, over thirty-five years in that laudable duty—Jefferson's scientific pursuits and accomplishments were, and still are, truly remarkable.

"Thomas Jefferson was born with a mind that was never still," wrote historian Silvio Bedini, "and a constant and insatiable curiosity." Growing up on the edge of the Virginia wilderness, and inspired by a father who was a talented surveyor and cartographer, his yearning for knowledge about the physical world—to fill in the blanks, so to speak, on nature's maps—knew no bounds. Education was the key to his wide-ranging mind, and his variegated accomplishments. "At the Reverend James Maury's school," wrote Bedini, "he first saw natural curiosities including fossils and geological specimens. . . ." Among his early philosophical, or scientific, mentors, Jefferson referred to Francis Bacon, Sir Isaac Newton, and John Locke as "the three greatest men the world has ever produced."

Another natural and moral philosopher proved tremendously influential. At the College of William and Mary, Dr. William Small of Scotland, according to Jefferson in his *Autobiography*, "probably fixed the destinies of my life." Small was "a man profound in most of the useful branches of science," penned Jefferson, "with a happy talent of communication . . . & an enlarged & liberal mind. . . . [F]rom his conversation I got my first views of the expansion of science & of the system of things in which we are placed." That "system of things" the author of the Declaration later explored to no end, and with great enjoyment.

In his day, Thomas Jefferson became the preeminent American patron, or cultivator, of science. During the early years of the republic, science was dominated by gentlemen amateurs such as Jefferson, men for whom the pursuit of science was an avocation. (It was not until the middle of the nineteenth century, in fact, that specialization and professionalism in science took over, and the word "scientist" came into wide usage.) "[Jefferson's] facts were not always right," wrote Edwin T. Martin, "nor his conclusions always correct. . . . There were times when he perhaps over-stressed immediate, utilitarian values. And certain of his preconceptions obscured his grasp of the truth." Nonetheless, over the course of his lifetime, Thomas Jefferson applied his analytical mind to such fields as agriculture, anthropology, archaeology, astronomy, botany, cryptography, ethnology, linguistics, mechanical inventions, meteorology, and paleontology. In several of these realms of science Jefferson's contributions were significant.

One such "realm" was archaeology. Even as a youth Jefferson had been fascinated by American Indians, or "aborigines" as he also called them. Of particular interest were the barrows they had left behind. Jefferson wrote about these in his *Notes on the State of Virginia*. (Modern editor William Peden called *Notes*—completed in December 1781 and revised the winter of 1783–84—"probably the most important scientific and political book written by an American before 1785.") In the chapter entitled "Aborigines," Jefferson recalled when "about thirty years ago" (or in the early 1750s), a party of Native Americans passed through Albemarle County seeking an old Monacan barrow, or mound, that was located near the site of Monasukapanough, one of their villages along the Rivanna. The Indians, he noted, "went through the woods directly to it, without any instructions or enquiry. . . ." It was obviously a repository of the dead, and Jefferson listed several opinions regarding it—as well as others located in Virginia—that had helped pique his curiosity: "Some have thought they covered the bones of those who have fallen in battles . . . [while some] ascribe them to the custom, said to prevail among the Indians, of collecting at certain periods, the bones of all their dead. . . . Others again supposed them the general sepulchers for towns. . . ."

This mound he determined to "open and examine . . . thoroughly." He failed to record the exact date of the dig, unfortunately, but the results were nonetheless impressive. According to Jefferson, the barrow "was of spheroidical form, of about 40 feet diameter at the base, and had been of about twelve feet altitude, though now reduced by the plough [*sic*] to seven and a half. . . . I first dug superficially in several parts of it, and came to collections of human bones at different depths, from six inches to three feet below the surface. . . . I proceeded then to make a perpendicular cut through the body of the barrow, that I might examine its internal structure. This passed about three feet from its center, was opened to the former surface of the earth, and was wide enough for a man to walk through and examine its sides. At the bottom . . . I found bones; above these a few stones . . . then a large interval of earth, then a stratum of bones, and so on. At one end of the section were four strata of bones plainly distinguishable; at the other, three; the strata in one part not ranging with those in another. The bones nearest the surface were least decayed. No holes were discovered in any of them, as if made with bullets, arrows, or other weapons. I conjectured that in this barrow might have been a thousand skeletons."

Jefferson's systematic excavation is important for a number of reasons. It was one of the first such archaeological digs on the North American continent. (It predated by over fifty years, in fact, the coining of the word "archaeology" in 1837.) And, by positing questions and then following an orderly, experimental procedure in order to answer them, Thomas Jefferson anticipated what became known in the 1850s as the "scientific method." In the case of this Albemarle County burial mound, he concluded that its skeletal occupants had not been killed in Native American conflicts nor had it been a village's common earthen crypt. "Appearances certainly indicate," he wrote, "that it has derived both origin and growth from the accustomary [*sic*] collection of bones, and deposition of them together."

More importantly, Jefferson's careful investigation of the mound featured an analysis of its layers, or "strata" as he referred to them. That reference is extremely significant. "As far as is known," wrote J. Jefferson Looney (editor of *The Papers of Thomas Jefferson: Retirement Series*), "he devoted one day in his entire life to excavations in the field, but during that day, and with no apparent precedent on which to draw, he invented the concept of stratigraphy. . . ." Although he was but an amateur archaeologist, Jefferson, wrote Peden "anticipated by a century the aims and methods of modern archaeological science." Modern-day archaeologists, in fact, refer to Thomas Jefferson as the "father" of the science.

His interest in Native Americans also carried over into linguistics. Thomas Jefferson was passionate about recording, and categorizing, their words and languages. "It is to be lamented . . ." he remarked in *Notes on the State of Virginia*, "that we have suffered so many of the Indian tribes already to extinguish, without our having previously collected and deposited in the records of literature, the general rudiments at least of the languages they spoke. Were vocabularies formed of all the languages spoken in North and South America, preserving their appellations of the most common objects in nature . . . with the inflections of their nouns and verbs . . . and these deposited in all the public libraries, it would furnish opportunities . . . to construct the best evidence of the derivation of this part of the human race."

In the 1790s, the American Philosophical Society—of which Jefferson had been a member since 1780—began accumulating Native American vocabularies. In this effort the Society was guided by Jefferson's concept of using comparative linguistics to map out the Indians' early history and migrations. His contribution, however, was more than theoretical. While serving as our nation's first secretary of state, according to Looney, Jefferson "personally took notes on the vocabulary of the Unquachog Indians by interviewing the twenty surviving members of that tribe [at the Pusspatock settlement near Brookhaven, Long Island], and he instructed explorers and badgered settlers and travelers to send him others. . . ." To that end, circa 1791 he had a form printed which listed over 250 standard English words followed by blank spaces for the recording of their Native American equivalents. Copies were distributed to anyone he thought likely to travel amongst the country's numerous native tribes.

Over the course of twenty years Jefferson continued this analytical study of aboriginal tongues, eventually accumulating over fifty basic vocabularies. "In this interest and in his recognition of the importance of linguistic evidence as the key to Indian pre-history," wrote Peden, "Jefferson was a pioneer both as anthropologist and philologist," (or one who studies historical and comparative linguistics). Unfortunately, the Sage of Monticello's wonderful collection was largely destroyed in transit from Washington to Albemarle County. What was left was submitted in 1817 to the American Philosophical Society.

Linguistically speaking, Jefferson was also something of a neologist, or creator of words. He surmised, wrote Monticello researcher Rebecca Bowman, that "[t]he process of coining new words . . . was the only way to give 'copiousness and euphony' to the language. . . . [H]e envisioned an elaborate history of English to prove that a language could never be too rich." He never compiled that history but still managed to leave his mark on the language itself. According to the *Oxford English Dictionary*, Thomas Jefferson was the first known user—in writing—of over seventy-five words. Many of them are either familiar terms or their easily understood variations. These include "authentication," "belittle," "commerciable," "continuable," "countervailing," "dischargeable," "discountable," "dutied," "inappreciable," "patricidal," and "unconciliatory." Perhaps surprisingly, in 1807 he also gave birth to the word "doll-baby" when he described "[t]he dresses of the annual doll-babies from Paris."

Naturally, many of Jefferson's word creations are rather obscure, such as "amovability," "amphibologism," "debarass," and "graffage." Not to mention "spathic"—meaning cleavable and lustrous—as in "[t]he property of the spathic acid," from a 1788 missive. The reader will probably not be surprised to learn that our Virginia neologist also begat four terms which were never used again (except, of course, in reference to his coining them): "Angloman," "enregistry," "intercollonnation," and "plexi-chronometer." For their non-use we should probably be grateful.

Another of Jefferson's words is "Megalonyx." It refers to the clawed animal he believed had been the original owner of the large, fossilized remains found by miners in Greenbrier County, Virginia. The bones had been excavated out of a saltpeter cave—from the depth of only two to three feet—in 1796. Sent to him by his friends

John and Archibald Stuart, the collection consisted of a small fragment of the femur, or thigh-bone; a perfect radius, or forelimb segment from the thumb side; another radius broken in two; three claws, and a half dozen other foot bones along with a few fragments. The Stuarts—who believed that the clawed monstrosity was a large lion—also sent Jefferson some incredibly tall tales which supported their presumption. Carved onto a rock alongside the Great Kanawha River, supposedly, was the perfect image of a lion, they wrote, and years earlier mountain folk had heard the thunderous roaring of a huge beast. This evidence—both physical and auditory—seemed to point to the same lion-like behemoth.

The bones and the stories excited Jefferson and he sent a brief description in July 1796 to astronomer and mathematician David Rittenhouse, president of the American Philosophical Society. (Unfortunately, Rittenhouse—the second head of that esteemed organization—had recently passed away.) Jefferson described the animal as belonging to "the family of the lion, tyger [sic], panther etc. but as preeminent over the lion in size as the Mammoth is over the elephant." After measuring his Greenbrier County bones, and comparing them with those of a standard lion, he wrote excitedly to Dr. Benjamin Rush: "What are we to think of a creature whose claws were eight inches long, when those of the lion are not 1 1/2 inches; whose thighbone was 6 1/4 [inches in] diameter, when that of the lion is not 1 1/2 inches?" What Jefferson thought was clear—*Megalonyx*, as he named it, was a carnivore over three times as large as the king of the jungle, big enough to bring down a mammoth! He notified the Society of his intention to present them the bones. Fellow member Benjamin Smith Barton—a physician and botanist—wrote back that an account of the amazing find would, no doubt, be "very acceptable" for the forthcoming volume of *Transactions*, the Society's publication.

Jefferson eagerly prepared his paper entitled "A Memoir of the Discovery of Certain Bones of an Unknown Quadruped, of the Clawed Kind, in the Western Part of Virginia." This, along with the fossilized bones themselves, Jefferson took to Philadelphia. Arriving on March 2—welcomed by the customary sixteen-gun salute—he immediately procured accommodations convenient to both Congress Hall and the American Philosophical Society headquarters. He was installed as the new Society president on March 3, and was sworn in as vice president of the United States the following evening. He was scheduled to present his *Megalonyx* paper on March 10.

Sometime during the intervening period, however, Jefferson received a shock. While perusing the Philadelphia bookstores he was startled to discover an account published in an English magazine of a very similar creature. This was especially obvious from the accompanying engraving of the enormous skeletal remains. Written by a young French naturalist, Georges Cuvier—who later gained fame in the new science of paleontology—the article described how the bones were found in Paraguay in 1789, carefully excavated, and transported to Spain. But the gargantuan Paraguayan was not a lion, it was not even a carnivore! "[I]ndeed," penned Jefferson, "it is classed with the sloth, ant-eater, etc., which are not of the carnivorous kinds; it was dug up 100 feet below the surface, near the river La Plata. The skeleton is now mounted at Madrid, [and] is 12 feet long and 6 feet high."

Chagrined, but no doubt grateful to have stumbled upon Cuvier's account, Thomas Jefferson hastily modified his *Megalonyx* paper. He scratched out the sections that unequivocally identified it as lion-like, substituting instead vague references of it being an animal of the "clawed kind." He also added a postscript which noted the similarities between his brute and Cuvier's great sloth—the *Megatherium*—but concluded that positive identification must await the unearthing of more of *Megalonyx's* skeleton, most notably its teeth. (Ironically, Jefferson would have been spared the embarrassment of altering his article if he had remembered that an early description of the *Megatherium*, along with an illustration, sat languishing in his files. He had received it years earlier while serving as minister to France.)

As with his work in archaeology, Jefferson's paleontological efforts placed him amongst that fledgling science's first practitioners. (The word "paleontology," in fact, was not coined until 1838.) After Jefferson's death in 1826, George Cuvier—by then France's most renowned scientist—praised the Virginian's "enlightened love for the sciences and . . . broad knowledge of scientific subjects to which he has made notable contributions." One hundred years later, early twentieth-century American scientists were even more complimentary. One, for example, called his *Transactions* piece the "signal gun of American paleontology." At about the same time— referring to his *Megalonyx* work and especially his later fascination with the *Mastodon* (discussed in another chapter)—Frederick Lucas and Henry Osborn dubbed Jefferson the "father of paleontology." While that moniker may be too laudatory—he had, after all, misidentified the Greenbrier County cave dweller—there's no question as to his rightful place among the pioneers of that science. In his honor, the massive Virginia ground sloth is known today as *Megalonyx jeffersonii*—Jefferson's "Great Claw."

Jefferson's *Megalonyx* memoir is interesting in another aspect— in it he argued against species extinction. Although a commonly held point of view at the time—Benjamin Franklin, for example, concurred—it was nonetheless one of the period's most controversial scientific disputes. First expounded by Jefferson in *Notes on the State of Virginia*, his argument against the extinction of species stemmed from the old "chain of being" notion which dated back to the Middle Ages. This hierarchical theory, according to Edwin T. Martin, regarded the created universe "as an infinite series of 'links' in a chain, running from inanimate nature and the very lowest order of being up through man, the angels, and God himself." As the "chain" represented harmony in the natural world, the loss of any one "link," according to the theory, would ultimately lead to chaos. How could the God of Nature allow any such thing to happen?

Jefferson's thoughts regarding extinction evolved over time but he never completely abandoned the chain-of-being concept. He used this theory to argue that the *Megalonyx*, as well as the *Mastodon*, could still be found somewhere in those uncharted areas of the American West. Republican congressmen Samuel L. Mitchill—a friend, supporter, and fellow amateur scientist—reflected the ongoing debate when he noted in his wonderful eulogy that: "[Jefferson] supports, of course, the notion that individuals of the Mammoth are yet alive. [Recently], a written communication was made to me from the Prairie du Chien, in which the respectable writer entertained a similar belief. The evidence, nevertheless, is far from conclusive. This enormous animal is now considered by the best judges to be extinct, as scores of other tribes are which have once been inhabitants of the globe."

Just as species extinction was debated, so were a large number of Jefferson's scientific pursuits. Much of this fault-finding can be traced to the growing antagonism between the Federalist and Jefferson's own Democratic-Republican parties. The rising criticism of Jefferson corresponded perfectly with his ascension to the presidency. "Controversy began to simmer hotly during Jefferson's Vice-Presidency," wrote Martin, "and it boiled over during the campaigns of 1800 and 1804." "Who could possibly want a philosopher-scientist as president of the United States?" asked Jefferson's detractors. "Not a soul," responded William Corbett (Federalist publisher of the Philadelphia-based *Porcupine's Gazette*), who added that "if one circumstance more than another could disqualify Mr. Jefferson from the Presidency, it would be the charge of his being a philosopher." Asbury Dickens wrote in 1800 that "[s]cience and government are two different paths. He that walks in one, becomes, at every step, less qualified to walk with steadfastness or vigour [*sic*] in the other."

Because of his fascination with the mammoth—the creature known today as the American *Mastodon*—President Jefferson was derisively nicknamed by the press "Mr. Mammoth." Having tickled the public fancy, the word began popping up everywhere. Federalists referred to Jefferson as a "mammoth infidel." A new-fangled gunboat he proposed for the Navy became a "Sea-Mammoth." For his love of Natural History, Jefferson was called a "feeder of prairie-dogs and bull-frogs." One satirist declared that Jefferson was working on a dissertation on cockroaches, while a young poet called the author of the Declaration a "wretch" who should resign his "presidential chair" in order to search for "horned frogs, 'Mid the Wild wastes of Louisiana bogs. . ."

In his *Knickerbocker's History of New York*, Washington Irving caricatured President Jefferson as a hypocritical, shallow know-it-all. "Of metaphysics," penned Irving, "he knew enough to confound all hearers and himself into the bargain." His logic was such that he "seldom got into an argument without getting into a perplexity."

One such "perplexity" was Jefferson's belief in the existence of an enormous salt mountain—said to be 180 miles long and forty-five miles wide—that supposedly sat 1,000 miles up the Missouri River. Jefferson had included a description of the saline range, provided him by trappers said to be reliable, in his report to Congress regarding Louisiana. "The existence of the salt mountain," wrote Martin, "became a matter of public debate, with the Jeffersonians as believers and the anti-Jeffersonians as doubters." President Jefferson was supposed to be a "philosophical" genius, said the Federalists—this story proved instead the amazing extent of his gullibility.

This attack in particular stung Jefferson, and made him quite a bit more cautious when it came to second-hand information. "It is well known that in December 1807," wrote Republican congressman Samuel L. Mitchill, "there was a descent of stones from the atmosphere to the earth in the towns of Fairfield, Weston, and Huntington, Connecticut, immediately consequent upon the explosion of a fiery meteor. My correspondents . . . who went [there], wrote me an account of their adventure, and sent me by the mail a specimen of the aerolite. . . . The curiosity of a senator who lodged at the same house as myself [in Washington] was worked to a high pitch. He had accepted an invitation to dine with the President that day; and he induced me . . . to lend him the letter and its accompaniment for communication to the philosopher of Montecello [*sic*]. He returned from the party indignant at the reception of his story. He said it . . . provoked a sort of scornful indifference: and that [Jefferson] said he could answer it in five words . . . *it is all a lie.* To my friend I replied, they had so imposed upon him in relation to the mountain of salt, that he seemed to be resolutely on his guard against a trick by a shower of stones."

During Jefferson's lifetime, Natural History—the study and description of nature—was an incredibly broad field covering such wide-ranging topics as the classification of birds, the methods of preserving dead animals, the use of electricity in promoting plant growth, the possibility of species extinction, the listing of the flora and fauna of the West, anthropology, and the burgeoning sciences of archaeology and paleontology. In Virginia, the most popular branch of Natural History was botany. Truly an activity for the masses, the pursuit of botany was also a possible pathway to wealth and a potential means for discovering new curative agents. "Botany I rank with the most valuable sciences," wrote Jefferson, "whether we consider its subjects as furnishing the principal subsistence of life to a man & beast, delicious varieties for our tables, refreshments from our orchards, the adornments of our flower-borders, shade and perfume of our groves, [or] materials for our buildings. . . No country gentleman should be without what amuses every step he takes into his fields."

An amusement, yes, but botany for Jefferson was also an extremely utilitarian science. Jefferson, wrote Peter Hatch, Monticello's director of gardens and grounds, "was fascinated by the practical applications to which the botanical world could be used. . . One might describe Jefferson as a 'hortobotanist' in the way he aspired to exploit the botanical world for useful and horticultural purposes." Once his love for this science was known, American correspondents sent him cotton tree seeds, a specimen of Missouri-grown wild hemp, indigenous Florida orange seeds, South Carolina grapevine leaves, moss retrieved from the hot springs in present-day Arkansas, as well as a bottle of salad oil—perhaps the nation's first—pressed in New York from Georgia-produced sesame seeds.

He also made every effort to bring to America any plant which might prove beneficial. From abroad came rutabaga seeds, a Chinese mulberry plant, a Maltese wintermelon seed, and—from the superintendent of the National Garden in Paris—a package holding 700 seeds, all from different plants. After receiving what he referred to as "precious" breadfruit seeds, Jefferson vowed to introduce the exotic tree into the Southern states. "One service of this kind rendered to a nation," he penned, "is worth more . . . than all the victories of the most splendid pages of their history, and becomes a source of exalted pleasure to those who have been instrumental to it." While Jefferson dispersed many of the plants sent him, he also experimented—in the "little mountain's" numerous gardens and groves—with an amazing assortment. "The staggering number of both useful and ornamental plants grown at Monticello, including over 300 vegetable and 170 fruit varieties," wrote Hatch, "attests to Jefferson's experimental approach. Monticello was a botanic garden of new and unusual introductions from around the world. . . ."

One particular foreign introduction—the Portuguese-born Abbé José Correia da Serra—arrived in the United States in 1812 and first visited Monticello the following year. But a few years later Jefferson offered Correia da Serra "a comfortable room" at Monticello whenever he desired it. (He became, in fact, the only non-family member to receive such an invitation.) What was the attraction? The well-educated and well-traveled European was also a scientist of international renown, a gentleman whom Jefferson described as the "best digest of science in books, men, and things that I have ever met with, and with these the most amiable and engaging character." During his numerous, extended visits to Monticello, the main topic of discussion was botany. "The world of plants, on which [Correia da Serra's] interest centered," wrote Dumas Malone, "was one in which his host was especially at home, and he was a man of universal knowledge after Jefferson's own heart." When not engrossed in some fascinating volume he and Jefferson were often seen wandering the slopes of Monticello Mountain.

Many of Jefferson's Natural History pursuits were directed at what he considered an incredibly important goal, a matter of national honor really—the refuting of the theories posited by French scientist Georges Louis Leclerc, the Comte de Buffon. Born in eastern France in 1707, Buffon became the keeper of the *Jardin du Roi* (the king's garden) and the director of the Royal Museum. A mathematician, biologist, and cosmologist, Buffon was an esteemed member of the royal Academy of Sciences and one of the first foreigners elected to the American Philosophical Society. Thanks to his comprehensive work in Natural History—his *Histoire naturelle, générale et particulière* (1749–1778) eventually filled forty-four volumes—he was considered by many to be the eighteenth century's leading naturalist.

Jefferson met with Buffon while serving as American minister to France, but he was already very familiar with the Frenchman's works and theories. Referring to Buffon in his *Notes on the State of Virginia* as "the best informed of any naturalist who has ever written," Jefferson had noted that: "One sentence of his [*Histoire naturelle*] must do him immortal honour [*sic*]. 'I love as much a person who corrects me in an error as another who teaches me a truth, because in effect an error corrected is a truth.'" If true to his word then the Frenchman, by all rights, should have become completely infatuated with the amateur naturalist from Virginia.

What infuriated Jefferson was Buffon's assertion that American flora and fauna—as well a human beings—were "degenerated" versions of Old World species. Jefferson summed up Buffon's arrogant, Eurocentric point of view, in his *Notes*, as follows: "1. That the animals common both to the old and new world are smaller in the latter. 2. That those peculiar to the new are on a smaller scale. 3. That those which have been domesticated in both have degenerated in America; and 4. That on the whole [America] exhibits fewer species."

In *Notes on the State of Virginia* Jefferson went after the world-renown naturalist with a passion, seeking to completely undermine his obnoxious theory. He tackled the first point with a table he called "A comparative View of the Quadrupeds of Europe and of America." Listing creatures varying in size from a 2.2-pound flying squirrel, of the European variety, to an 1,800-pound American buffalo, Jefferson concluded "that of 26 quadrupeds common to both countries, 7 are said to be larger in America, 7 of equal size, and 12 not sufficiently examined." This table, he wrote, "impeaches the first member of the assertion. . . ." He attacked Buffon's second notion with another table—one which arranged "the animals found in one of the two countries only"—and noted that "there are 18 quadrupeds peculiar to Europe [and] more than four times as many, to wit 74, peculiar to America. . . ." The fact that the first creature on the American list—the tapir, at 534 pounds—"weighs more than the whole column of Europeans . . . disproves the second member of the assertion. . . ." With a third table Jefferson showed that domesticated New World animals—given "equal food and care"—were just "as large as the European stock from which they are derived . . ." and wrote that the lists taken all together illustrated that America actually contained more, not fewer, species.

Once Jefferson was in France, his printed disagreements with Buffon spilled over into their face-to-face encounters. During one conversation, Jefferson—knowing that Buffon believed that the New England moose and the European reindeer were one in the same—boasted to the Frenchman that "the reindeer [of Europe] could walk under the belly of our moose." When Buffon scoffed at the notion Jefferson vowed to prove it true. To do so he enlisted the aid of Maj. Gen. John Sullivan, then serving as president of New Hampshire, who, wrote Jefferson, "made the acquisition an object of a regular campaign. . . . The troops he employed sallied forth . . . in the month of March—much snow—a herd attacked—one killed— in the wilderness—a road cut twenty miles—to be drawn by hand from the frontiers to his house. . . ." The arrival in Paris of the bones and skin of a rather large moose—along with the other items Sullivan sent: the horns of caribou, elk, and deer—seemed worth to Jefferson the startling expense, sixty guineas. "I really suspect you will find that the moose, the round-horned elk, and the American deer, are species not existing in Europe," Jefferson penned to Buffon in his note accompanying the precious cargo. One can almost hear Jefferson snickering as he continued: "I wish these spoils, Sir, may have the merit of adding anything new to the treasures of nature, which have so fortunately come under your observation. . . ." Buffon promised to correct his errors but unfortunately died a few months later, in April of 1788.

Astronomy, climatology, and meteorology, in Jefferson's day, fell under the broad heading of Natural Philosophy. (Encompassing today's Physical Sciences, Natural Philosophy included—as Jefferson noted in planning the department for the University of Virginia—the "laws and properties of bodies generally, including mechanics, statics, hydrostatics, hydraulics, pneumatics, acoustics, optics and astronomy.") Jefferson's appreciation of astronomy was probably fueled by his facility with mathematics, and his love for meticulous accuracy. As he had noted: "No two men can differ on a principle of trigonometry." Prior to the Revolution, he had envisioned constructing a large observatory—featuring a 107-foot-tall tower—atop Montalto, a mountain overlooking Monticello. It was never built but Jefferson's sketches remain. Over the years he purchased a number of expensive astronomical instruments, including various telescopes and a portable orrery, or clockwork model of the solar system. For the interior of the Rotunda's dome, at the University, he proposed a planetarium which was to be "painted sky-blue and spangled with gilt stars in their position and magnitude copied exactly from any selected hemisphere of our latitude." Unfortunately, this plan too never saw the light of day.

Jefferson felt that an understanding of the make-up of the universe was valuable. Astronomy's main use to him, however, was in the enhanced accuracy it provided to surveyors and mapmakers. "[T]he bulk of [Jefferson's] writings on astronomy," wrote Looney, "are preoccupied with the use of celestial observations to pinpoint more accurately one's position on the globe."

In the field of meteorology Thomas Jefferson was probably the best-informed American alive. His fascination with this science originated in his student days in Williamsburg where he came into contact with Francis Fauquier, the colonial governor. An avid meteorologist, Fauquier—who had penned an account of an unusual Virginia hailstorm for the Royal Society of England—probably gave Jefferson his first ideas about the regular recording of valuable meteorological data. In his own *Weather Memorandum Book*—which he began using on the Fourth of July, 1776—Jefferson meticulously recorded his observations, with but a few understandable lapses, for the next fifty years. "My method is to make two observations a day," he wrote, "the one as early as possible in the morning, the other from 3. to 4. aclock [*sic*]. . . ." These observations included the temperature, and a brief description of the weather conditions— both jotted down twice a day—as well as miscellaneous comments "such as the appearance of birds, [the] leafing and flowering of trees, [and] frosts [that occurred] remarkably late or early. . . ."

Jefferson became a one-man weather bureau. "Friends wrote for information which he supplied from his own multitudinous records," wrote Martin, "or from data he had collected from other sources." Frontier scientist William Dunbar, for example, sent him in 1801 a year's worth of weather observations made at his home near Natchez, Mississippi. Dr. Hugh Williamson mailed him similar information from Quebec. Jefferson's goal in recording this data was extremely utilitarian. By thoroughly understanding the climate of each section of the United States—its temperature, prevailing winds, and annual rainfall, etc.—local farmers would best know what vegetables to plant, and when to plant them.

As with many men of great fame, Thomas Jefferson over the years has garnered several laurels that are not rightly his. One of these is the title of being a "great inventor." A brief list of the mechanical objects often attributed to his incredibly fertile mind includes the portable copying press, the polygraph, and the spherical sundial, as well as the simple machines actually built into Monticello itself: automatic double doors, wine bottle dumbwaiters, and the revolving serving door. Unfortunately, the master of Monticello invented none of these gadgets. The copying press, for example, was the invention of James Watt—an English-born genius with many devices to his name—who patented it in 1780. Traveling overseas, Jefferson required a portable version so he had a model made in London "on [the] principles of the large one" he owned. Far from inventing the portable copying press, Jefferson simply took his press to a workman—a mechanic—and asked him to make it smaller. Watt himself, in fact, manufactured a portable version soon after patenting the original. The invention of the polygraph— or letter copier—made the copying press obsolete. This machine was actually the work of John Isaac Hawkins in conjunction with the ubiquitous Charles Willson Peale, a mechanical genius. Their American patent dates to 1803. President Jefferson purchased two polygraphs, tinkered with them, and then wrote the inventors with suggested improvements. These were incorporated. He did not invent the polygraph—which he called "the finest invention of the present age"—but he helped make it better.

Thomas Jefferson built a spherical sundial at Monticello in 1809. Sitting on top of a miniature column, it consisted of a whitewashed globe—10.5-inches in diameter—with an attached orbiting ring which cast a thin shadow onto a hopefully correct longitudinal timeline. Spherical sundials, also called armillary-spheres, date back to the first century A.D. Vitruvius—a Roman writer—first laid down the theoretical foundation for spherical sundials in his famous work on architecture entitled *De Architectura*. Perhaps not surprisingly, Thomas Jefferson—architecture aficionado that he was—had a French translation of Vitruvius's tome at Monticello, and was fond of quoting from it. In a letter to architect Benjamin Latrobe, Jefferson described his contraption in minute detail, concluding with a revealing admission: "Perhaps indeed this may be no novelty." Jefferson did not invent the spherical sundial, but he can be credited with introducing a 1700-year-old device into the United States.

As to the gadgets installed at Monticello: Jefferson got the idea for the automatic double doors—which, no doubt, he was fond of showing off—from a book, while wine bottle dumbwaiters, which brought wine up from the cellar, he saw prominently displayed in a famous Parisian restaurant: the Café Mécanique. Along with the revolving serving door—which he first saw in a monastery—these were all devices Jefferson admired, and had built into the fabric of his home, after learning about them somewhere else. Not really the inventor of a long list of practical items, Jefferson was instead a gadgeteer. Over the decades, during the evolution of Monticello and into his seventeen-year-long retirement, Thomas Jefferson collected gadgets recently invented by others, reintroduced gadgets invented in the ancient world, and adapted gadgets he had seen elsewhere for his personal use.

Did Thomas Jefferson invent anything? He considered agriculture "a science of the very first order." One of the two items Jefferson created from whole cloth was a perfected plow, one he called the "mould board of least resistance." After observing European designs, and noting their deficiencies, he resolved to create a moldboard—the curved plate above the plowshare—that would lift and turn the desired depth of sod with the least expenditure of energy. In his own words his moldboard would "receive the soil after the share has cut under it . . . raise it gradually, and . . . reverse it." Designed mathematically, Jefferson's invention was field-tested beginning in 1793. Five years after retiring from the presidency, Jefferson began casting his moldboards in iron. In 1815 he noted that his invention was "so light that the two small horses or mules draw it with less labor than I have ever before seen necessary. It does beautiful work and is approved by everyone." Although it is unclear how many farmers used Jefferson's moldboard it was featured in James Mease's *Domestic Encyclopedia*, published in Philadelphia in 1803. Additionally, the invention won for Jefferson the French Society of Agriculture's gold medal.

Thomas Jefferson's other invention was a wheel cipher, a cryptographic machine used to code and decode military messages. Jefferson invented the wheel cipher while serving as our nation's first secretary of state, between 1790 and 1793. The creation consists of twenty-six wooden coin-shaped wheels, each threaded onto a central iron rod. As each wheel has inscribed on its edge the letters of the alphabet it's easy to see how revolving these wheels scrambles and unscrambles words and phrases. Jefferson apparently stopped using his wheel cipher after 1802, but it was re-invented—reborn so to speak—just prior to World War I by the United States Army. Simple in its construction, and simple to use, this version was employed until the beginning of World War II. Its creation—and, of course, Jefferson's detailed description of it—led some to name him the "father of cryptography."

What was the engine driving all of Jefferson's scientific pursuits? His insatiable curiosity. A lifelong learner—he wanted to know everything about everything—Jefferson learned many different ways: from his travels, his readings, and his conversations with guests at Monticello. Because Thomas Jefferson was but an amateur scientist—a status, in fact, he was always willing to acknowledge— one has to wonder what else he might have accomplished if he had not spent over thirty-five years in public service. Nonetheless, the author of the Declaration was a brilliant scientist who corresponded with virtually all of his period's most notable "philosophers," took to task the world's greatest living naturalist, penned essays for America's leading scientific organization, collected data on a daily basis, dug into the earth searching for answers, founded several sciences himself, and turned his own home into a veritable museum.

Thomas Jefferson's scientific legacy is immense. His early use of the scientific method, for example—his emphasis upon objectivity and the gathering of data before reaching conclusions—set the standard for others to follow. "Jefferson's orderly habits of mind and meticulous record keeping," wrote Looney, "are inspiring, if daunting." His promotion of science—while serving in office—gave that branch of learning an inestimable boost. He believed that scientific progress would ultimately lead to human happiness, and did much to further research and expand scientific knowledge. As president of the American Philosophical Society for seventeen years, from 1797 to 1814—twelve years of which he was in national office—Jefferson served on numerous commitees and advisory groups, and secured many learned papers and natural history specimens. His insistence upon the freedom of the scientific mind—"his boundless faith in free intellectual inquiry" according to Looney—is impossible to quantify but also impossible to overstress. It cast light where darkness had prevailed. "I am among those who think well of the human character generally," he wrote in 1799. "I believe also . . . that [man's] mind is perfectible to a degree of which we cannot as yet form any conception. It is impossible for a man who takes a survey of what is already known not to see what an immensity in every branch of science yet remains to be discovered. . . ."

Harvard professor Donald Fleming referred to Jefferson as "a universal man who put his learning to the service of an enlightened nationalism. Americans would never look upon his like again."

William Clark (1770–1838).

VI

"SEARCHING FOR THE BONES OF THE MAMMOTH":
Jefferson & Big Bone Lick, Kentucky

"[T]he most extraordinary depository of bones of the great hoofed animals of the Glacial Age in America."

- John Uri Lloyd

Once the formal negotiations had been completed, the lanky Virginia governor escorted the Lenape warriors into an elegant side-room, a salon well decorated with blue silk draperies, engravings, and an abundance of portraiture. One by one the Delaware braves followed, their top-feathers bending beneath the doorframe as they strode into the luxurious chamber. The place was a rented home in Richmond, Virginia: the time, the early spring of 1781.

Taking a seat in one of the room's many chairs, Virginia's chief executive motioned for the Lenape to do the same. They declined. Instead they stood clustered before him, their red and black-patterned blankets pulled tight around their brown shoulders. Flashes of brightly beaded bandoliers sparkled from underneath the folds of their sun-dulled woolen capes. How greatly they contrasted the "civilized" individuals that hung from the walls surrounding them, staring at them.

They waited quietly for the freckled white man to explain the stern faces framed in wood. Rather than introducing the Delaware Indians to these evident leaders of the white world, however, the governor instead displayed an all-encompassing interest in the Lenape world: their civilization and customs. Through an interpreter he inquired of their territory and their villages. He asked about their rivers, their methods of fishing, the game they pursued, and how they prepared their meat. To their responses he listened closely, attentively, and watched in obvious delight as the translator slowly recounted their words.

And then the redheaded governor leaned forward, his hazel eyes wide in anticipation. "Do you know, or have you heard, of the Mammoth," asked Thomas Jefferson, "the creature whose huge bones have been found at the Saltlicks, on the Ohio? Have you seen this animal?"

"Their chief speaker immediately put himself into an attitude of oratory," Jefferson wrote a short time later in his *Notes on the State of Virginia*, "and with a pomp suited to what he conceived the elevation of the subject" related a tradition "handed down from their fathers.... [I]n ancient times a herd of these tremendous animals came to the Big-bone licks," said the Lenape warrior throwing his blanket back and exposing his right arm, "and began a universal destruction of the bear, deer, elks, buffaloes, and other animals, which had been created for the use of the Indians."

"[T]he Great Man above," he continued with a wave of his hand toward the ceiling, "looking down and seeing this, was so enraged that he seized his lightning, descended on the earth, seated himself on a neighboring mountain . . . and hurled his bolts among them till the whole were slaughtered, except the big bull, who presenting his forehead to the shafts, shook them off as they fell; but missing one at length, it wounded him in the side; whereupon, springing round, he bounded over the Ohio, over the Wabash, the Illinois, and finally over the great lakes, where he is living" to this day.

Thomas Jefferson failed to record his reaction to the Lenape oral tradition, but the aborigine's tale obviously aroused his interest in the "Saltlicks on the Ohio"—the amazing, otherworldly site in Kentucky also known as Big Bone Lick. The large fossils uncovered there fascinated him, especially those of the colossal beast he referred to as the "mammoth," the animal known today as the "Mastodon." And he believed that large herds of the American *Mastodon* could still be found thundering across the unexplored west. Jefferson instructed Meriwether Lewis and William Clark to be on the lookout for these creatures during their 1804 to 1806 expedition and he sent Clark to Big Bone Lick in 1807 with the express purpose of digging up some of the fossilized remains. The success of that venture made Jefferson an important figure in the early days of vertebrate paleontology.

Big Bone Lick, Kentucky, is located in the northernmost section of the Bluegrass State, within a broad loop of the Ohio River, about twenty-three miles southwest of Cincinnati. It lies along Big Bone Creek which flows into the mighty Ohio, but a few miles to the west. English geologist Charles Lyell, writing about the region in 1845, described it as one of "flat table-lands intersected by valleys of moderate depth," valleys often containing bogs, and salt and mineral springs known as "licks."

"The term Lick is applied . . . to those marshy swamps where saline springs break out," wrote Lyell, "and which are frequented by deer, buffalo, and other wild animals for the sake of the salt, whether dissolved in the water, or thrown down by evaporation in the summer season, so as to encrust the surface of the marsh. Cattle and wild beasts devour this incrustation greedily, and burrow into the clay impregnated with salt, in order to lick the mud."

The enormous "wild beasts" that inhabited North America in epochs long past found the Kentucky salt springs just as enticing. What was it that drew them? Trace elements in the salt such as selenium, magnesium, tungsten, and iron: elements that instinct told them they must have to benefit their appetite, fertility, and growth.

During the late Ice Age, or late Pleistocene period (approximately twelve to fourteen thousand years ago), great sheets of ice covered the continent north of the Ohio River Valley. As the ice progressed southward large numbers of bison, ground sloths, and giant mammoths and mastodons—driven into the area—came to Big Bone Lick and slowly waded into the marshy ground. In their eagerness, however, dozens of these big creatures found themselves mired, and perished. "The heavy mastodons and elephants seem . . . to have pressed upon each other," wrote bluegrass state geologist Willard Rouse Jillson, "and sank in these soft quagmires of Kentucky."

The bog at Big Bone Creek must have been particularly attractive to the mastodons because at one point in time their fossilized remains seemed to be everywhere. "It is supposed that the bones of mastodons found [at Big Bone Lick] could not have belonged to less than one hundred distinct individuals," wrote Jillson.

What were these lumbering creatures? According to vertebrate paleontologist C. Bertrand Shultz the name *Mastodon*—from the Greek "mastodont," meaning "nipple tooth"—usually refers to the *Mastodon americanus*, or "American Mastodon," and its relatives of the Ice Age. They were primitive elephants—similar to the "Woolly Mammoth," but not shaggy—with short jaws and long tusks. "Mastodonts were typically browsers," wrote Shultz, "and ate leaves, bark, and even small branches of trees and shrubs." Some stood as tall as ten feet at the shoulder and weighed 11,000 pounds.

Thomas Jefferson probably first learned of Big Bone Lick in 1766. That year, wrote Ann Moore Lucas, "he met Dr. John Morgan in Philadelphia who had collected 'mammoth' . . . specimens from it." Imagine Jefferson's amazement as Morgan handed him an obvious animal molar the size of a melon. But Dr. Morgan was not the first white man to take an interest in the Kentucky salt lick. Writing in 1936 Willard Rouse Jillson surmised that the first European to view the amazing site was the French Canadian soldier and explorer Capt. Charles Lemoyne de Longueil, who descended the Ohio in 1729. Jillson believed that de Longueil had been shown Big Bone Lick "by the Indian guides who accompanied him." The local Native Americans, Jillson wrote, "relied upon this centrally located spring for much of the salt and a good deal of they game which they required. Up the broad, well-marked buffalo path . . . they came making regular visitations to this old salty bog to stalk with ease the great hoofed beasts. . . ." Celebrated French mapmaker Jacques Nicolas Bellin labeled Big Bone Lick, on his 1744 *Carte de la Louisiane*, as "the place where they found the elephant bones in 1729."

The English came to the region a few years later. Indian trader Robert Smith saw Big Bone Lick in 1744. Col. Christopher Gist followed in 1751, under the aegis of the Ohio Land Company of Virginia. From the salt marsh Gist brought back two teeth, one of which he described as hefting "better than four Pounds Weight." The next year Big Bone Lick was visited by picturesque John Findley, the backwoodsman later renown for guiding Daniel Boone into the heart of *Kentucke* in 1769.

"Mary Inglis, usually accredited as the first white woman in Kentucky," wrote Jillson, "while an Indian captive visited Big Bone Lick on a salt-boiling expedition with a party of Shawnees and three Frenchmen in the autumn of 1756." In order to affect an escape Inglis traded for a tomahawk with a Frenchman who, according to Richard Collins, was "sitting on one of the big bones cracking walnuts."

Many of the early descriptions of Big Bone Lick—those written in the 1760s and 1770s—are simply astounding. They seem to pertain to Africa, or India, rather than North America. Col. George Croghan, who ventured down the Ohio in 1765 as an Indian agent for the colony of Pennsylvania, kept a travel journal of his experiences. "In our way [to the lick] we passed through a fine timbered clear wood," he wrote. "[W]e [next] came into a large road which the Buffaloes have beaten, spacious enough for two wagons to go abreast, and leading straight into the Lick. It appears that there are vast quantities of these bones lying five or six feet under the ground, which we discovered in the bank, at the edge of the Lick. We found here two tusks above six feet long; we carried one, with some other bones, to our boats, and set off."

Unfortunately, this early fossil collection was lost just a week later when the colonel's party was set upon by a band of eighty Kickapoo and Mascoutin Indians. The determined Croghan and his men escaped, and the colonel himself returned the following year accompanied by a military entourage which included Capt. Harry

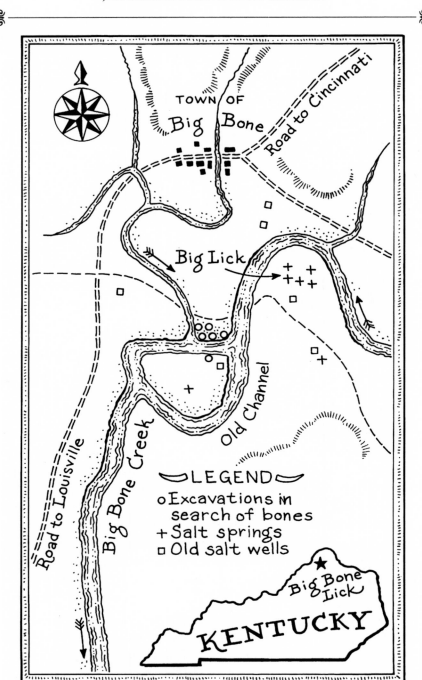

Big Bone Lick, Kentucky, as it appeared in 1831.
(*Map by the author.*)

Self portrait by Charles Willson Peale entitled
"The Artist in His Museum."
Note the Mastodon jawbone in the lower-right hand corner.

Gordon. "We encamped opposite the great lick," penned Gordon, an engineer officer, "and [on the] next day I went with a Party of Indians and Batteau-Men to view this much-talked-of Place. . . . [O]n our Arrival at the Lick . . . we discovered laying about many large Bones, some of which [were] the exact Patterns of Elephants Tusks, & others of different parts of a large Animal. The extent of the Muddy part of the Lick is 3/4 of an acre; this Mud being of a salt quality is greedily lick'd by Buffalo, Elk & Deer, who came from distant parts, in great Numbers for this purpose; we picked up several of the Bones, some out of ye Mud, others off the Ground. . . ."

In 1775 Nicholas Cresswell described Big Bone Lick as "a large muddy pond, a little more than knee deep with a Salt spring in it which I suppose preserves the bones sound. Found several bones of Prodigious size, I take them to be Elephants, for we found a part of a tusk, about two feet long, [and] Ivory to all appearance. . . . All of us stripped and went into the pond to grabble for teeth and found several."

Jefferson's interview with the Lenape braves, as noted above, took place six years later, in 1781. He related their incredible oral legend in his famous *Notes on the State of Virginia*, followed by a four-page discussion of the mammoth, or *Mastodon*, the creature he referred to as "the largest of all terrestrial beings." The "skeletons of unparalleled magnitude" are found in great numbers "on the Ohio, and in many parts of America further north," he wrote. Jefferson listed the monstrosity as native to North America, and correctly identified it as a distant relative of the elephant, one that had adapted to the colder northern clime.

He also thought it possible that they still roamed the western plains. Why? Considered alongside some of the other yarns being told of the uncharted west, the concept of living and snorting *Mastodons*—moving about in loud, dust-raising herds—might not seem so absurd. William Dunbar, for example, sent Jefferson an account of a giant New Mexico water-serpent, and Jean Baptiste Le

Moyne Bienville wrote of the existence, out west, of unicorns. Silver ore, it was rumored, could be found there in large, solid masses. And tall mountains of salt, supposedly, piled up alongside brackish streams. More importantly, however, because of the Enlightenment precept known as "chain of being," Jefferson, though scientific in his thought, simply could not accept the idea of extinction.

"It may be asked why I insert the Mammoth [on a chart of living creatures] as if it still existed?" the governor of Virginia mused in his *Notes on the State of Virginia*. "I ask in return, why I should omit it, as if it did not exist? Such is the œconomy of nature, that no instance can be produced of her having permitted any one race of her animals to become extinct. . . ."

"Once *Notes on the State of Virginia* was available in the United States in 1787," wrote Lucas, "Jefferson's interest in fossils became widely known. For more than two decades [he] received fossils from friends and acquaintances who knew of his curiosity." One year later the American Philosophical Society put together a committee—including Jefferson, Charles Willson Peale, and the renowned Dr. Caspar Wistar—that listed as its first priority the procurement of "one or more entire skeletons of the Mammoth. . . ." As president, Jefferson was true to that desire when—on June 20, 1803—he wrote to Meriwether Lewis outlining the goals for Lewis's upcoming journey to the Pacific coast. Under the heading of "Other object[s] worthy of notice" the author of the Declaration included "The animals of the country generally, & especially those not known in the U.S." and "the remains and accounts of any which may [be] deemed rare or extinct."

But the results of the Lewis and Clark Expedition were fairly disappointing, at least as far as the *Mastodon* was concerned. Stopping briefly on his westward trip down the Ohio, Lewis visited Big Bone Lick. He wrote Jefferson a detailed letter about the site—using 2,000 words, for example, to describe "a tusk of an immense size"—and sent back a box full of fossils. Unfortunately, this crate was lost somewhere along the way. On their 1804 to 1806 expedition, Lewis and Clark searched for the mastodon, "but encountered no herds," wrote Shultz, "nor even fragments of extinct ones."

President Jefferson remained undaunted. The return of Lewis and Clark in 1806 freed up those proven backwoodsmen for further undertakings. The next year Jefferson dispatched William Clark to Big Bone Lick on an expedition he financed out of his own pocket. The primary objective was the retrieval from the Kentucky salt marsh of the *Mastodon* bones required by Peale to complete a skeleton he was assembling in Philadelphia. Especially needed were the fossilized remains of the head and feet. "I have been employed two weeks at this place with *ten* hands searching for the bones of the Mammoth &c. without meeting with as much suckcess [*sic*] as I expected," the faithful Clark—who was not much on spelling—wrote Jefferson on September 20, 1807 from "Camp Big Bone Lick." "This Lick has been pillaged so frequently that but fiew [*sic*] valuable bones are to [be] found entire. I have found part of several *heads* of the Mammoth, tho most of them so decayed, that when the soft mud was taken from them and the air admited, they crumbled and fell to pieces. I have saved *Two* which are tolerably hard, also a part of the great *pan* of the head covering the brains. I have several pieces of the *Jaw bone* with the *Teeth* in them, and one with a *Small Tusk*. I have also found many of the *Teeth* and a part of a *jaw bone* of which I believe to be the Seberian Eliphant [*sic*] with *two teeth* in it. . . ."

In a follow-up missive dated November 10, Clark wrote of the "great Numbers of the Nighbours [*sic*] Cattle and horses, and sometimes hogs eagerly Comeing [*sic*] into the Lick and drinking an emence quantity of the water. . . ." When he inquired of the "Nighbours" they expressed the opinion that "there was something in the air about the Lick very agreeable to the Cattle," and that a drove of beeves "when in 2 and a half miles of the Lick . . . became restless and ran with eagerness to the Place and drank profusely. . . ."

Of course, the expedition—called by some the first organized paleontological dig in the United States—was not without its troubles. "This Lick is in a Valley serounded [sic] with hills," explained Clark, "the atmosphere Cold and damp. I had for the first time in my life, the Rheumatism in My wrists, shoulders, hips and knees dureing the time I remained under the influence of the Vapour arriseing [sic] from the Lick, and several of the men who worked in the water were slightly attacked with a chill and fever."

In the end, however, William Clark's expedition was a tremendous success. "It netted over 300 bones of various species," wrote Lucas, "including the coveted 'mammoth' cranium."

Anticipating their imminent arrival in Washington, Jefferson—on December 19, 1807—sent a letter to fellow Society member Dr. Wistar, at the time considered the nation's fossil expert. "Take your lodgings at the tavern close by us," Jefferson wrote anxiously. "Mess with me every day, and in the intervals of your perlustrations of the city, Navy Yard, Capitol, etc., examine these bones, and set apart what you would wish for the society. I will give you notice when they arrive here, and then you will select a time when you can best absent yourself for a week from Philadelphia. I hope you will not deny us this great service. . . ."

The precious cargo of fossils finally reached Washington on March 7, 1808, and Jefferson immediately renewed his invitation to Dr. Wistar. It was not until late June, however, that the learned scientist managed to make his visit. When he arrived at the White House, Wistar found that the president, in his glee, had spread the bones across the floor of a large room. In his spare time he had already begun organizing them. Jefferson intended to divide the collection into three parts: one for the National Institute in Paris, one for the American Philosophical Society, and another for his personal "cabinet" at Monticello.

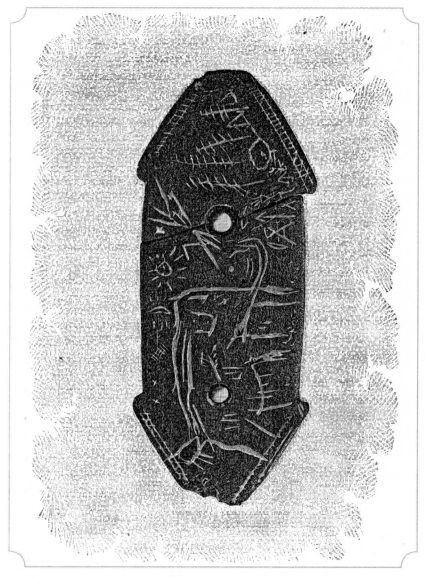

**The famous Lenape Stone discovered in Bucks County, Pennsylvania,
in the later part of the nineteenth century.**

Note that the images—particularly the lightning bolts directed at the head of the
mammoth or Mastodon—conform to the Lenape, or Delaware Indian, legend related
to Jefferson when he was governor of Virginia.

Wistar spent the better part of early July compiling a detailed report on the collection, and setting aside three boxes-worth to be shipped to Paris. "There the fossils became part of the Museum of Natural History," wrote Lucas, "where they became critically important to the study of paleontology in France." "The specimens selected by Wistar to complete the collection of the American Philosophical Society," penned Howard C. Rice, Jr., "found their way in due course to the Society's cabinet in Philadelphia." In 1849, over fifty of these bones were transferred to that city's Academy of Natural Sciences.

"The fossils which Jefferson reserved for his own collection," wrote Rice, "were taken to Monticello where they occupied a prominent place among his curiosities." They were exhibited in his museum-room, his wonderfully eclectic Entrance Hall. Jefferson must certainly have delighted in displaying fossils from Big Bone Lick to his visitors. "On [one side of the room], among many other striking matters," wrote George Ticknor in 1815, "was the head of a mammoth, or as [French paleontologist, Georges] Cuvier calls it, a mastodon, containing the only *os frontis* [or frontal bone], Mr. Jefferson tells me, that has yet been found." The following year the Baron de Montlezun reported seeing, at Monticello, a mammoth's head "formed of the upper jaw, which is perfect, and two halves of the lower jaw coming from different specimens." He also wrote that Jefferson had laid, side-by-side, mastodon and elephant teeth in order to illustrate how much they differed.

After Thomas Jefferson died his prized Kentucky bones were moved to the University of Virginia and put on display in the Rotunda. "No record of the fossil collection at the university exists after 1848," wrote Lucas, "and many surviving specimens today remain unidentified." In 1987, however, a few dusty fossils were found in the basement of the Virginia Museum of Natural History in Martinsville. Clay samples taken from these bones were tested against soil samples from Big Bone Lick. They matched.

The bog at Big Bone Creek was—and is—an amazing place, a place unlike any other in the United States. "Big Bone Lick," wrote Jillson, "was the very evident place of [the] death and entombment of many of the largest mammals that ever coursed the American wilderness." It captured Thomas Jefferson's imagination when first he heard of it—much like it trapped the big beasts—and held it fast until he could satisfy his curiosity, with an organized dig, over forty years later. Because of his fascination with fossils, and the unselfish way in which he disseminated the results of Clark's expedition, Thomas Jefferson is often considered the founder of vertebrate paleontology in North America.

The 1789 Jefferson bust by Jean Antoine Houdon (1741–1828).
(Photo by Jennifer Law Young.)

VII

"EMPIRE OF LIBERTY":

Jefferson & the American West

"Westward the course of empire takes its way. . . ."
- *George Berkeley, 1752*

On January 18, 1803, Thomas Jefferson submitted a secret message to the "Gentlemen of the Senate and of the House of Representatives." It marked the beginning of the fulfillment of one of his biggest dreams—the creation of a continent-wide "Empire of Liberty."

"The river Missouri, and the Indians inhabiting it," penned the fifty-nine-year-old president, "are not as well known as is rendered desirable by their connexion [*sic*] with the Mississippi, and consequently with us. It is, however, understood, that the country on that river is inhabited by numerous tribes, who furnish great supplies of furs and peltry to the trade of another nation. . . .

"An intelligent officer, with ten or twelve chosen men . . . might explore the whole line, even to the Western Ocean, have conferences with the natives on the subject of commercial intercourse, get admission among them for our traders, as others are admitted, agree on convenient deposits for an interchange of articles, and return with the information acquired, in the course of two summers. Their arms and accoutrements, some instruments of observation, and light and cheap presents for the Indians, would be all the apparatus they could carry. . . ."

According to Jefferson, the sum of $2,500 "for the purpose of extending the external commerce of the United States," would cover the entire undertaking. The expedition he envisioned would eventually cost quite a bit more but its rewards would be well-nigh immeasurable.

Thomas Jefferson is regarded by many as the "father of the American West." Part of the case behind this title is the Louisiana Purchase—the 1803 land acquisition that nearly doubled the size of the nation—but part, too, is the wildly successful Meriwether Lewis and William Clark expedition (1804–06). Jefferson, of course, was the intellectual force behind this epic trek which captured the public's imagination and focused it firmly on the Louisiana Territory and its seemingly limitless possibilities. Prior to the expedition the western wilderness "was a blank," wrote historian Bernard DeVoto, "not only on the map but in human thought. . . . [Lewis and Clark's journey] was the first report on the West, on the United States over the hill and beyond the sunset, on the province of the American future." Just as with any major undertaking, however, its eventual success underplayed, and even masked, everything that had gone before it—all of Jefferson's dreaming and planning, and all of his prior unsuccessful attempts. For Thomas Jefferson, the Lewis and Clark expedition was the culmination of a long and wearisome passage—one fraught with a number of failures.

Jefferson, unlike most of the Americans of his generation, began thinking of the West at an early age. That mind-set is not difficult to understand. He was born in 1743 at Shadwell—his father's plantation—in western Goochland County. (The very next year Albemarle County was carved from this section of the central Piedmont.) In 1743 this was *the frontier*—what was then the westernmost outpost of English civilization in Virginia. Thomas Jefferson grew up, therefore, in a wilderness, or backwater, part of the colony. Spending his childhood scrambling over the Southwest Mountains—of which Monticello is a part—within sight of the majestic Blue Ridge but twenty-five miles to the west, it is easy to imagine Jefferson wondering what lay beyond.

Another early influence was his father. A slaveholding planter and a member of the House of Burgesses, Peter Jefferson (1708–57) was also a successful surveyor and cartographer, or mapmaker. "In 1746," wrote Guy Meriwether Benson, "he and Thomas Lewis surveyed the 'Fairfax Line.' This assignment required an arduous expedition. . . . [I]n 1750 the Board of Trade and Plantations in England authorized the acting governor to appoint 'the most proper and best qualified' surveyors to complete a new map of Virginia. [Mathematics professor] Joshua Fry and Peter Jefferson were commissioned to carry out this order. Although they completed their map in 1751, it was first published in 1754 by Thomas Jefferys of London." A valuable representation of the Old Dominion, the 1751 Fry-Jefferson map went through several editions—the last seeing print in 1794—and was used by John Evans when he prepared his "Map of the Middle British Colonies." A reduced version also appeared in a 1756 atlas by the French royal cartographer, Gilles Robert de Vaugondy. As a youngster Thomas Jefferson took great pride in the fact that his father had produced the first accurate map of the colony of Virginia, at that time the most populous colony. "Jefferson," noted biographer Noble E. Cunningham, Jr., "owed his lifelong interest in exploration to his father."

Jefferson's westward point-of-view was also influenced by another gentleman—one who has been frequently overlooked—Dr. Thomas Walker. Born in 1715 in King and Queen County, Virginia, Walker became a successful physician, surveyor, and merchant. In the early 1750s Walker moved his family to Albemarle County and constructed Castle Hill alongside the Southwest Mountains. Possessing a vigorous constitution, in 1748 Thomas Walker accompanied an expedition into the Holston River Valley of Southwest Virginia. Two years later Doctor Walker—as agent of the Loyal Land Company of Virginia—led a small group of adventurers over the Alleghenies into Kentucky. The party spent a week near the headwaters of the Cumberland River before returning. The 900-mile round trip produced many valuable geographical results—the most important being the discovery of the Cumberland Gap and its approaches. Over the following fifty years, Daniel Boone and tens of thousands of other pioneers traveled Doctor Walker's path into Kentucky and the Ohio country.

Walker was a close friend of Peter Jefferson's, and his medical advisor. Upon the elder Jefferson's death in 1757, Walker became the administrator of his estate and fourteen-year-old Thomas Jefferson's guardian. He also tutored young Jefferson in his early studies. Walker's wealth of experience in the trans-Allegheny west and his interest in the sciences have been credited, in fact, with fostering many of Jefferson's later pursuits. The well-educated Walker, a gifted raconteur, must have enthralled Thomas with his stories of bear and buffalo hunts, and his many encounters with Native Americans.

(Incidentally, Walker was slated to head another expedition in 1753. "Some persons," wrote the Rev. James Maury, one of Jefferson's teachers, "were to be sent in search of that river Missouri in order to discover whether it had any communication with the Pacific Ocean; they were to follow the river if they found it, and [write] exact reports of the country they passed through, the distances they traveled, what worth of navigation those rivers and lakes afforded, etc." Much grander in scope than that into Kentucky, the plans for it were scrapped when the French and Indian War intervened.)

Jefferson's early life on the frontier and his exposure to men who had traveled out beyond the safe havens of white civilization cultivated in him a fascination with the wild lands to the west. Thanks to this early interest—and perhaps because he never traveled further west than the Shenandoah Valley—Jefferson became a voracious consumer of books on geography. Throughout his life he sought out, and acquired, books on the American Continent. While posted as minister to France (1785–89) Jefferson wrote that he had searched all of the principal Parisian bookstores and purchased "everything which related to America." In 1815—as he was about to sell his library of 6,700 books to Congress—one visitor to Monticello noted that, "The collection on [the America's] is without question the most valuable in the world." According to Benson, "No one knew more about the geography of North America in his own day than Thomas Jefferson."

Another factor in Jefferson's fixation with the West was the fact that, during his lifetime, America's frontier was continually being pushed westward. New areas were being opened-up and settled, new discoveries were being made, new information was being added to the maps of the continent. Nowadays, with perfect hindsight, it's easy to think of the West as the Louisiana Territory plus the states of the Southwest—broadly stated, "the land beyond the Mississippi River." The West to Jefferson, however—and the few other westward-thinkers of his generation—was continually morphing, evolving, expanding. Naturally, the West began just past the settlements along the eastern seaboard. Every successive expedition, every new detail regarding the soil and the abundance of game shoved the West further out. To Jefferson's father, for example, the West had been the Piedmont and Appalachian country, the area just beyond "the Most Inhabited part of Virginia" (as reads the cartouche of the 1751 Fry-Jefferson map). To Dr. Thomas Walker—the man who in 1750 discovered the Cumberland Gap—the West was southwestern Virginia and eastern Kentucky.

Daniel Boone's expeditions across the Appalachians (1769–71) and his founding of Boonesboro in 1775 pushed the imaginary western boundary yet again. (Jefferson later became acquainted with Boone in 1781 when he was governor of Virginia and the legendary backwoodsman was a member of the Virginia legislature.) "By the time of the American Revolution," wrote historian James P. Ronda, "the West meant what is now Ohio, Indiana, and Illinois. This was the West that George Rogers Clark [of Albemarle] and his intrepid Virginians seized from the British" in 1778–79. In thought, however, Jefferson was already ahead of the curve. Clark and his 175-man army had proved that determination meant more than numbers in the vast wilderness. It was during the American Revolution that Jefferson began thinking of the West as the vast region of North America which, during his lifetime, had flown the flags of France and Spain—the trans-Mississippi.

Among the general American populace, the formation of the Republic following the Revolution marked a watershed period in their thinking about the West. That change in thought—the seemingly simple process of the people turning 180 degrees from the East to the West—can be traced by studying the evolution of word usages. Prior to 1776, for example, according to historian David Hackett Fischer, "the frontier was known as the 'back settlements,' or the 'backcountry'. . . . The fact that colonists thought of it as the 'back' rather than 'front' of their world tells us which way they were facing. That usage changed suddenly and very broadly in the early years of the Republic. The earliest recorded use of *frontier settlement* was in 1789; *frontier man*, 1782; *frontiersman*, 1814."

Jedidiah Morse (1761—1826) described this transformation of thought and what had brought it about. A graduate of Yale College, Morse became a Congressional clergyman and the writer of a number of books on geography. Many have considered him, in fact, the "father of American Geography." In the preface of his immensely popular 1784 school textbook—entitled *Geography Made Easy*—Morse noted that: "There is no science better adapted to the capacities of youth . . . than Geography. . . . This part of education was long neglected in America. . . . We humbly received from Great-Britain our laws, our manners, our books, and our modes of thinking; and our youth were educated as British subjects, not as they have since been, as citizens of a free and independent nation. The Revolution has proved favourable [*sic*] to science in general among us; particularly to that of the Geography of our own country."

Thomas Jefferson could not have agreed more—geography was a science, an invaluable one when it came to North America. It was his refined knowledge of geography that placed him at the forefront of thought about the migration of Americans westward. Ever patriotic and very nationalistic, Jefferson saw clearly—better than anyone—the importance of the West to the future of America. This is typified by his "Empire of Liberty" vision. "Our confederacy,"

Jefferson penned prior to the adoption of the Constitution, "must be viewed as the nest from which all America, North or South, is to be peopled." He later wrote that people "speaking the same language, governed in similar forms, and by similar laws" would eventually settle the entire continent. "In an age of imperialism," wrote historian Stephen E. Ambrose, "he was the greatest empire builder of all. His mind encompassed the continent. . . . [H]e thought of the United States as a nation stretching from sea to sea. More than any other man, he made that happen."

Jefferson began putting his "Empire of Liberty" vision to work with the Northwest Ordinance of 1787. Often regarded as Congress's most significant achievement under the Articles of Confederation, the Ordinance—of which Jefferson was one of the principal authors—allowed for the admission into the Union of several states from the Northwest Territory. (This was the region north of the Ohio and east of the Mississippi that had been secured from the British by George Rogers Clark. Following the Revolution several states—principally Virginia—had ceded their claims to the region to the Federal government.) "These [new] states would be fully equal to the original thirteen," wrote Ambrose. "Thanks to Thomas Jefferson, the United States would be an empire without colonies, an empire of equals."

While the Old Northwest was being peopled, the trans-Mississippi, according to Jefferson, would accommodate the Native Americans displaced by the advancing whites. Across the great water the Indians would, hopefully, take up farming and become civilized—Europeanized. Along with many eighteenth-century social theorists, Jefferson believed that human societies moved through—or advanced through—various stages of development. The earliest humans, according to Jefferson, were hunters "living under no law but that of nature . . . covering themselves with the . . . skins of wild beasts." The next level, like "those on our frontiers," were "raising domestic animals to supply the defects of hunting." These were followed by farmers, which Jefferson called "the pioneers of the advance of civilization" and, lastly, the "most improved state" of humankind—urbanites like those living in the seaport towns. Obviously, following Jefferson's logic, the American Indians had quite a lot of improving to do. Eventually, however, they would become a part of the body politic. Hopefully they would be ready by the time the United States—having incorporated everything east of the Mississippi—was ready to embrace the balance of the continent. That time, Jefferson knew, was rapidly approaching. Even a river as mighty as the Mississippi could not stem the tide of humanity longing for new lands.

The Mississippi, "the father of waters," had first been sighted in 1519 by the Spanish explorer, Alonso Álvarez de Pineda. Other Spaniards, Alvar Núñez Cabeza de Vaca and Hernando de Soto, encountered the great river during explorations in the mid-1500s. Frenchmen Jacques Marquette, a Jesuit missionary, and Louis Jolliet—setting out from the Great Lakes—explored the Mississippi's upper reaches including the mouth of the Missouri River, in 1673. The Indians told them that up the Missouri, and beyond an easy portage, lay a southwest-flowing river that emptied into the western sea. Nine years later, in 1682, another Frenchman—René-Robert Cavelier, Sieur de La Salle—sailed down the Mississippi to its mouth. It was La Salle who claimed for France the entire Mississippi Valley. He named the territory *Louisiane* in honor of King Louis XIV.

"Over the next forty years," penned Benson, "French explorers, traders, miners, and missionaries explored the upper Mississippi, Ohio, Red, and Arkansas rivers and, most importantly, the Missouri River." In 1713 Etienne Véniard de Bourgmont pushed up the Missouri as far as its confluence with the Platte River (near today's Omaha), but for more than seventy years afterwards no European ventured further. In the southwest, however, the French reached the Rio Grande in 1713 and Sante Fe—founded in 1610 by the Spanish—in 1739.

Along the Gulf coast, Pierre Le Moyne d'Iberville had headed three French expeditions—the first in 1699—that constructed small fortifications near modern Mobile, Alabama, and Biloxi, Mississippi. In 1718 the French colonial capital for Louisiana was established at New Orleans. The French understood that the powerful Mississippi would inevitably become the trade and colonization corridor for the entire central section of the continent. By controlling the maw of this mighty river, they hoped to connect their northern settlements with those on the Gulf of Mexico.

It was there—on the Gulf of Mexico as well as in east Texas—that French and Spanish interests collided. Frenchman La Salle had established a colony, Fort Saint Louis, at Matagorda Bay in southeastern Texas in 1685. Determined to eradicate this threat, the Spanish launched an expedition against it. Arriving in 1689 the Spaniards discovered that disease and Indian attacks had already accomplished their goal: but few French colonists remained. In 1718, while the French were founding New Orleans, a Spanish expedition trekked through east Texas and began setting up missions. The following year—coincidental to a short, Franco-Spanish war—French troops attacked those settlements putting the missionaries and tiny garrisons to flight. In 1721 the Spanish in turn drove the Frenchmen from east Texas.

In the northern tier of the American West, however, France faced no competition. Setting off from Canada, Pierre Gaultier de Varennes, Sieur de La Vérendrye, in 1739 arrived at the Great Bend section of the Missouri River, the very spot where the Lewis and Clark Expedition wintered amongst the Mandan people sixty-five years later. "Thus, by the time the French period in North America came to an end with the fall of Quebec in 1759," noted Benson, "the French had explored most of the territory that lay between" the Appalachians and the Rockies. Similarly the Spanish, by the mid 1700s, had trekked across much of the Southwest in search of gold.

The West, therefore, had been "explored" somewhat and mapped somewhat—although incorrectly—but very few people truly grasped the immensity of the North American interior, or even understood all of its "wonderful productions"—as wrote scientist William Dunbar—its plants, animals, and minerals. Born in Scotland, Dunbar had attended universities in Glasgow and London before coming to America in the 1790s. "Dunbar had a plantation called 'The Forest' in the hills near Natchez," penned historian Dan L. Flores, "where he constructed one of the outstanding early astronomical observatories in North America...." Introduced to Jefferson as "the first Character in this part of the World" when it came to science, Dunbar wrote of the region's "most fertile lands" which "will hereafter support a prodigious population." To Jefferson, this aspect of the West, the commercial possibilities, were of tremendous importance. As scientific information trickled back to him it further piqued his interest.

Sometimes the information was less than reliable. Such was the case with a 1763 tome Jefferson purchased entitled *The History of Louisiana, or of the Western Parts of Virginia and Carolina.* Originally published in Paris in 1758, it was the work of Antoine-Simon Le Page du Pratz, a French military engineer. Le Page du Pratz had lived in present-day Louisiana from 1718 until 1733 and had undertaken a five-month journey up the Mississippi River on foot. In the narrative, he describes the Indians—"Naturals" he calls them—as well as the buffalo, partridges, and pheasants that his party dined upon. He provides details on the area's many "wonders" including beaver dwellings, lead-ore, and gypsum which was easily extracted from the side of a hill. But he also claims that he saw "tigers" roaming the banks of the Mississippi. Le Page du Pratz's book also features a map of Louisiana which—although showing the lower Mississippi and lower Missouri rivers fairly accurately—depicts an easy route to the Pacific via the "Beautiful River." This path had been described to the Frenchman by one of the Naturals.

Other explorers, too, originated all sorts of tall tales about the strange creations that existed in the sparsely peopled region. French adventurer Bénard de La Harpe, for example—representative of the Mississippi Company—journeyed up the Red River and in 1719 founded France's most westerly trading post near today's Texarkana. La Harpe kept a detailed journal of his travels—the discovery of which over eighty years later generated quite a stir. In it he reported that "unicorns" could be seen in the Southwest. Jean Baptiste Le Moyne Bienville, the founder of New Orleans, also wrote of the existence of the beautiful single-horned creatures.

In some locations out west brackish springs bubbled up from below, some said, and the salt piled high in tall mountains. Many believed that the huge American *Mastodon*, a cousin to the mammoth, still thundered across the plains in massive, fearsome herds. Jefferson had seen *Mastodon* bones, and had heard of their existence from the Lanape Indians. He was inclined to believe that the behemoths still lived because of his belief in the then-prevalent "chain of life" theory. "Such is the economy of nature," he noted, "that no instance can be produced of her having permitted any one race of her animals to become extinct. . . ."

Though a scientist, even Dunbar fell prey to some of the west's fantastical tales. In 1801 he penned a letter to Jefferson describing a massive New Mexico "water-serpent." Dunbar, of course, had not seen the slithering monster himself. Another story that the Scotsman passed along to Jefferson told of large solid masses of metal, supposedly "silver ore," sitting on the ground waiting to be retrieved. According to Flores, this account originated with the "iron-nickel meteorites on the Southern Plains." The Native Americans venerated them as "extraordinary manifestations of nature" and used them as "Medicine Rocks."

Jefferson finally got involved in promoting the exploration of the trans-Mississippi just after the Revolution drew to a close. His first attempts, however, ended in frustration. Mere weeks following the war's conclusion—in December of 1783—he heard a disturbing rumor. British entrepreneurs, he penned Gen. George Rogers Clark, had "subscribed a very large sum of money for exploring the country from the Mississipi [sic] to California. They pretend it is only to promote knolege [sic]. I am afraid they have thoughts of colonising [sic] into that quarter. Some of us have been talking here in a feeble way of making the attempt to search that country. . . . How would you like to lead such a party?" Clark wrote back with several suggestions. A small party of three or four—rather than Jefferson's idea of a full-scale military expedition—"might perhaps compleat [sic] your wishes at a Trifling Expence [sic]." It would also have the advantage of not alarming the Indian nations. Though full of ideas, however, Clark had neither the time nor the finances to mount such a expedition.

In 1785, while posted as minister to France, Jefferson heard that Louis XVI was mounting an expedition to the Pacific Northwest to be led by Jean-Francois de Galaup, Comte de La Pérouse. "They give out that the object is merely for the improvement of our knowledge," Jefferson wrote to naval hero John Paul Jones. "Their loading . . . appear to me to indicate some other design; perhaps that of colonising [sic] on the West coast of America. . . ." First the British and now the French! In Jefferson's mind both European nations were eager to settle the trans-Mississippi, thus wresting from his grasp this long dreamed-about gem. (The Spanish, of course, were already there but their power, Jefferson knew, was waning.) Inquiring after French intentions, Admiral Jones discovered that the La Pérouse expedition, fortunately, was bound instead for the South Pacific.

The following year Jefferson made another stab at reconnoitering the American West—one that bordered on the bizarre. "While I resided in Paris," the Virginian wrote, "John Ledyard, of Connecticut arrived there.... He had accompanied Captain [James] Cook on his [1776–80] voyage to the Pacific ocean, and distinguished himself ... by his intrepidity. Being of a roaming disposition he was now panting for some new enterprise." Panting indeed, the idea for this "enterprise" was bold in the extreme. Jefferson offered Ledyard funds and his personal support if he would "go by land to Kamschatka [in other words, walk across Europe to Eastern Siberia], cross in some of the Russian vessels to Nootka Sound [on Vancouver Island, in Western Canada], fall down into the latitude of the Missouri [meaning, hike 200 miles south into present-day Washington State], and penetrate to, and through, that to the United States. [Ledyard] eagerly seized the idea, and only asked to be assured of the permission of the Russian government." That Jefferson was able to procure.

Ledyard subsequently set out on foot from Paris—with only his dog as company—and made it, as winter was setting in, to within two hundred miles of Kamschatka. There, unfortunately, wrote Jefferson, "he was arrested by an officer of the empress [Catherine], who by this time had changed her mind, and forbidden his proceeding." The overzealous provocateur was put into a carriage, driven to the Polish border, and pushed out on the other side. Ever eager to make use of an energetic romantic like Ledyard, Jefferson wrote the Rev. James Madison in 1788 that the adventurer might be induced to "go to Kentuckey [sic], and endeavor to penetrate Westwardly from thence to the South Sea." Unfortunately, poor Ledyard committed suicide in Egypt that same year.

In 1792, Jefferson along with other members of the American Philosophical Society tried to raise funds to underwrite a botanical expedition up the Missouri River by Pennsylvania botanist, Moses Marshall. Trained as a physician, Marshall had abandoned his medical practice in order to assist his uncle—the better-known botanist, Humphry Marshall—in his burgeoning horticultural business. The younger Marshall was eager to take up the project but, unfortunately, this plan too came to naught.

Enter French naturalist and adventurer André Michaux. Having arrived in America in 1785, in 1792 Michaux proposed to the American Philosophical Society that he lead a party up the Missouri River. After crossing the western mountains—which everyone expected to be paltry—and gaining the Pacific, the Frenchman would return with no small amount of valuable scientific and commercial information. Impressed by the scheme—and Michaux's credentials—Society members George Washington and Alexander Hamilton, as well as Society Vice President Thomas Jefferson, pledged funds to make it a reality. "I readily add my mite to the [project]," he wrote, "and do authorize you to place me among & upon a footing with the respectable sums which may be subscribed."

By January 23, 1793, the Society was able to promise one thousand pounds to whomsoever had the pluck to pull off the overland excursion. Eighteen-year-old Meriwether Lewis, then in Charlottesville on army business, "warmly solicited" Jefferson for the honor of heading-up the expedition. He even agreed to execute the plan with only one companion so as not to unduly alarm the Native Americans. The nod, instead, went to Michaux who, after all, had made the initial proposal. Michaux was given extensive instructions by Jefferson before setting off down the Ohio River. He was, for example, to "take notice of the country you pass through, it's general face, soil, river, mountains, it's productions animal, vegetable, & mineral so far as they may be new to us . . . the names, numbers, & dwellings of the inhabitants, and such particularities as you can learn of them." The main purpose according to Jefferson, however, was altogether different—Michaux was to discover "the shortest and most convenient route of communication between the United States and the Pacific Ocean." There was one other minor detail—because Louisiana was Spanish, Michaux should traverse the Mississippi well to the north to "avoid the risk of being stopped."

Michaux set off in June of 1793. After traveling but a short distance, however, according to Jefferson, "he was overtaken by an order from the minister of France . . . to relinquish the expedition, and to pursue elsewhere the botanical inquiries on which he was employed by that government. . . ." Once again, Jefferson was disappointed.

A decade later, however—during Jefferson's first term as president—fate conspired to make the exploration of the American West a realizable goal. France, in 1762, had given Louisiana to Spain. Comprising 828,000 square miles, Louisiana stretched from the Mississippi River to the Rockies, from Canada to the Gulf of Mexico. In 1800 Napoleon Bonaparte convinced the Spanish to cede the huge region back to France. When President Jefferson heard rumors of this retrocession—realizing that Napoleon planned to establish an empire in North America—he reacted with alarm writing that it was "impossible that France and the U.S. can continue long friends when they meet in so irritable a position."

Fortunately for the future of the United States, a war over Louisiana was not to be. In France, American ministers were negotiating for the purchase of the city of New Orleans and Western Florida (the southern portions of present-day Alabama and Mississippi). They were authorized to pay a bit over nine million dollars. But the French—thwarted in their efforts to get an army into the North American West, and expecting a renewed war with England—offered, instead, to sell all of Louisiana. With the treaty signed on May 2, 1803, the Louisiana Territory changed hands, and the American nation was doubled—all for the price of fifteen million dollars. Jefferson's "Empire of Liberty" was now a part of the United States.

Part of his dream—the acquisition of most of the West—had been achieved, the next step was detailed exploration.

The Cabinet, or study, at Monticello.
(Photo by Bruce Young.)

VIII

THE FREEMAN & CUSTIS EXPEDITION:
"the Lewis and Clark of the South"

T he natural beauty of the surroundings belied the fact that a confrontation was imminent. On either side of the meandering river the gently rolling grasslands extended for miles—all beneath a boundless canopy of blue. Here the river, wrote Thomas Freeman, "was confined between banks 200 yards apart, and nearly 30 feet high, in which the narrow stream, occupying not more than one third of the space, pursued a serpentine direction between level sand beaches." From the river's red clay banks rose thickets of heavy timber and cane. The location was a section of the Red River in present-day Bowie County, Texas. The date was July 29, 1806.

Along the river's northern shore the American party, numbering forty-seven, was engaged in preparing dinner, their boats beached on the reddish sand. Around the numerous campfires the tension was palpable. Native American runners had brought word that a large Spanish force was moving against them. If they resisted, the Spanish commanding officer, said the Indians, intended to "either kill them," according to Freeman, "or carry them off [as] prisoners, in irons." For several days the expedition had been aware of the Spaniards' proximity. Firing had been heard upriver and, this very morning, Indian scouts had located the nearby camp of the Spanish advance guard. On receiving this information, the American's had halted their boats, taken out and examined their weapons, and readied them for use at a moment's notice.

Soon after the exploring party commenced dinner, a detachment of 150 Spanish horsemen, led by four officers, wrote Freeman, "advanced in a full gallop . . . along the beach towards us. As soon as they reached the water, and were about crossing to the side on which the Americans were, the men were ordered to ascend the bank and range themselves along it in the cane brake and bushes. . . ." Thus concealed in a defensive position inaccessible to cavalry—and instructed to fire when the sentinels on the beach below fired—they were prepared to give the Spanish a severe reception. As a further precaution, noted Freeman, "a non-commissioned officer and six privates were pushed along the bank as to be in the rear of the Spaniards, when their attack should be made."

"The Spanish Column," penned Freeman, "passed on at full speed through the water, and came on towards the party. The Sentinels, placed about 100 yards in advance of the barges, hailed them according to orders, and bid them to halt. They continued to advance with the apparent determination to charge. The sentinels a second time bid them halt, cocked their pieces, and were in the act of presenting to fire, when the Spanish Squadron halted . . . at about 150 yards from the sentinels." With the opposing forces thus arrayed—and the strong possibility of war hanging in the balance—the elaborately uniformed Spanish officers cantered forward to parley.

Most Americans are familiar with the story of the Meriwether Lewis and William Clark Expedition—how the intrepid explorers set off from St. Louis with their Corps of Discovery in May, 1804, and, after reaching the Pacific in November of the following year, returned to their departure point in September of 1806. Few, however, have even heard of another, major expedition that President Thomas Jefferson dispatched into the Southwest. Led by Thomas Freeman and Peter Custis, and accompanied by U.S. soldiers and French and Native American guides, this "Grand Excursion"—as it was called by Secretary of War Henry Dearborn—journeyed up the Red River from the Mississippi for over 600 miles. According to historian Dan L. Flores, "it was the largest and, in terms of original appropriation, the most expensive American exploring expedition of the age."

On February 19, 1806, President Jefferson submitted to Congress his first report on Lewis and Clark's progress. While the message relayed the valuable information thus far collected by the ongoing expedition—Lewis's statistical survey of the Plains Indians, for example, runs to some sixty pages—it also unveiled a bit of Jefferson's larger plan for Louisiana: it stated his intention to explore the Red River. The president's larger plan, it is important to understand, included the investigation of *all* of the western streams that flowed into the Mississippi River. He was more immediately concerned, however, with the Mississippi's principal tributaries, the Missouri, which of course Lewis and Clark were investigating, and the main streams south of that river—the Arkansas and the Red.

Initially, Jefferson's proposal for these two rivers involved, as he wrote William Dunbar in March, 1804, sending a party up the Arkansas to its source, "thence along the highlands to the source of the Red river [in other words portaging the boats], & down that to its mouth. . . . These surveys will enable us to prepare a map of [Louisiana] which in its contours and main waters will be perfectly correct." Dunbar—who lived on a large plantation outside of Natchez, in the Mississippi Territory—was a Renaissance man much like Jefferson: his serious interests included astronomy, botany, medicine, and western exploration. For a decade the two corresponded about matters relating to the Southwest. The president's purpose in writing Mississippi's "pioneer scientist" was to get him to direct the combined Arkansas-Red expedition.

"By locating the sources of these two affluents of the Mississippi," wrote historian Isaac J. Cox, "[Dunbar's] expedition would mark two important points on the 'undoubted' limits of Louisiana. . . . Meanwhile, the general public might become better informed regarding their new possession and the President and his advisors gain the necessary information to guide them in settling its boundaries with Spain." Therein lay the rub—the Louisiana Territory's southwest boundaries were still undecided. The French believed that the province included Texas while the Spanish, citing expansion under their rule, proclaimed that the Arkansas River was Louisiana's southern border. Dunbar, in his reply to Jefferson, warned that the Spanish would probably use military force to halt any Red River expedition that attempted to proceed upriver beyond Natchitoches. Another problem was posed by a splinter band of the Osage nation, one known to be unfriendly toward Americans. Having recently moved to the Arkansas, these hostiles would likely oppose any movement along that stream.

Still, Dunbar was interested in supporting the president—having written "It will give me great pleasure . . . to promote the proposed expedition on the Red and Arcansaw [sic] rivers"—and Jefferson was eager for events to move forward in the Southwest. So, while Jefferson worked "to remove Spanish impediments," Dunbar explored the Ouachita (pronounced "Wash-uh-taw") River accompanied by a small contingent of soldiers and Dr. George Hunter of Philadelphia, a scientific reinforcement sent out by the president. Rising in south-central Arkansas, the Ouachita flows almost due south until flowing into the Black River and thence into the Red about thirty miles upstream from that river's confluence with the Mississippi.

Dunbar and Hunter set out from Natchez in mid October, 1804, and returned by the end of January. In the process they explored over 300 miles of the Ouachita, traveling all the way to Hot Springs in present-day Arkansas. Naturally, they encountered problems. As Dunbar later reported to Jefferson, the scow-like "Chinese" boat Hunter had designed proved insufficient, and the lack of a commissioned officer made the soldiers difficult to control. More importantly, Dunbar bemoaned that neither he nor Hunter were naturalists and made several arguments against the idea of portaging—or hauling boats overland—from one river to another. Nonetheless, useful information had been garnered. Indeed the exploring party, wrote Flores, "became the first scientific expedition to report back from Louisiana." Dunbar and Hunter's meticulous journals provided some of the earliest accounts of the Ouachita River Valley's flora and fauna as well as the Hot Springs' first detailed chemical analysis. The president was a bit gratified over the results—he referred to the Ouashita as "an interesting branch"—but the fact remained that Dunbar and Hunter had surveyed merely a "branch," not a main artery.

Steadfast when a project piqued his interest, Jefferson continued to push for further expeditions into the Southwest. And, taking into account Dunbar's recommendations, he now began focusing on the Red River. Just over 1,000 miles long, the Red River rises in today's eastern New Mexico, flows eastward across the Texas Panhandle—becoming the boundary between that state and Oklahoma—then, after turning south in southwestern Arkansas, crosses into Louisiana and eventually enters the Mississippi River. When Jefferson learned in early 1805 that Congress was adding an additional $5,000 for exploration—the initial appropriation for Lewis and Clark's venture had been half that amount—the president urged Dunbar to proceed with plans for a Red River expedition. "The work we are now doing is, I trust, done for posterity, in such a way that they need not repeat it," Jefferson wrote Dunbar. "We shall delineate with correctness the great arteries of this great country. Those who come after us will . . . fill up the canvas we begin."

Finding trained scientists to lead the excursion proved very problematic. Both Hunter and fifty-six-year-old Dunbar turned Jefferson down. So, too, did the famous naturalist William Bartram, then sixty-five and infirm. Two other men recommended by Jefferson—surveyor Seth Pease, and a Mr. Wily who taught in a Washington academy—were uninterested. The choice of George Davis, a mathematician then working in New Orleans, was vetoed by Dunbar, who wrote that the young man was a very "improper person." Turkish-born Constantine Samuel Rafinesque, a respected albeit eccentric botanist, at first volunteered to accompany the party but instead sailed for Europe. Ornithologist Alexander Wilson also volunteered, via the U.S. mail, but—as the president never responded—the letter was most likely lost.

Enter Thomas Freeman. Born in Ireland, Freeman was a surveyor and a civil engineer who had traveled to the United States in 1784. His early years have been lost to history but it is certain that they featured an excellent education. "As early as 1792," wrote Flores, "he may have been employed as surveyor and inspector of the port in Plymouth, Massachusetts, and in 1794 had been commissioned by President George Washington as a surveyor of the new capital city on the Potomac." It was there that he possibly rubbed elbows with Jefferson, as well as with Alexander Hamilton, Washington's treasury secretary. Following his work in the new-born Washington, Freeman surveyed the boundary between the U.S. and Spanish Florida and, in 1803, accompanied Indiana Territorial Governor William Henry Harrison up the Wabash River to confer with the region's Native Americans.

In the spring of 1805, Freeman corresponded with Jefferson regarding celestial observation. The president, no doubt, was impressed, and—perhaps remembering Freeman from his work in the capital—offered him the leadership of the "Grand Excursion" in August or September of that year. Dunbar, initially apprehensive about the choice, wrote Jefferson that "I am glad to learn . . . that Mr. Freeman comes to take direction of the expedition up the red river."

But first there must be planning! Called to Washington in November, Thomas Freeman passed an evening with Jefferson, at which time he was given the president's typically detailed exploring instructions and, as noted Flores, "a letter of introduction and a draft to purchase a compass, a chronometer, and other scientific instruments in the mathematics shops of Philadelphia." Then it was off to that city for two months of training under mathematician Robert Patterson, naturalist and physician Benjamin Smith Barton, and portrait painter and general Renaissance man Charles Willson Peale—all of whom had worked with Meriwether Lewis. "I shall set out for Red River & etc. to Explore Louisiana," Freemen wrote to John McKee. "I expect to take with me a Naturalist and an assistant astronomer if such persons properly qualified can be found here willing to hazard travel in the Neighborhood of [Santa Fe]. . . . Great many difficulties, and some personal danger will attend the exploration, but, I will—"Stick or go Through" The more danger the more honor."

The honor of heading the expedition, of course, Freeman would have to share. And naturally, following Dunbar's advice, Jefferson's preference was for a naturalist. Peter Custis was born in 1781 on the Virginia Eastern Shore and was related by marriage to many of the Old Dominion's most prominent families, including the Randolphs, Lees, and Washingtons. "A solid secondary education," wrote Flores, "had prepared him to enter the medical and natural history program at the University of Pennsylvania in 1804, where he became a student and protégé of Barton." Although a trained naturalist— having absorbed from Barton the rudiments of botany, zoology, and taxonomy, or scientific classification—he lacked practical experience. Custis received his appointed to the expedition on January 14, 1806—three days later he and Freeman departed Philadelphia for the Mississippi river town of Natchez.

To lead the exploring party's military detachment Jefferson chose Capt. Richard Sparks, a Pennsylvanian who had spent a portion of his youth with the Shawnees. An able hunter and backwoodsman, Sparks was the commanding officer at Fort Adams, a post on the east bank of the Mississippi sixty water miles south of Natchez and but a few miles above the mouth of the Red. Fort Adams also supplied Sparks's second in command, Lieut. Enoch Williams, who would assist Freeman in taking celestial readings. The balance of the original military contingent included two non-commissioned officers, seventeen privates, and—like the Lewis and Clark expedition—an enslaved African American. Guides and interpreters were to be added later.

Outfitting a large expedition was no small feat. The requirements included the basic food stuffs—the necessities they did not expect to encounter on the journey—weapons and ammunition, vessels for transportation, etc. In the case of the Freeman and Custis Expedition, however, one simple fact made this task easier—some five thousand dollars worth of necessary goods, leftovers from the Dunbar and Hunter trek, were made available in Natchez. These items included various medicines, hundreds of flints, and barrels of gunpowder, as well as trinkets for the Native Americans. More importantly, the leftovers featured scientific instruments—a barometer (for fixing altitude), a chronometer (or timepiece), a microscope, two thermometers, a camera obscura (for assisting with illustration), and a telescope (for determining latitude).

To help with classifying the Red River flora, Custis, according to Flores, "seems to have carried with him" Linnaeus's *Systema Vegetabilium*, "a one-volume, thousand-page botanical compendium of all the known plants of the world," and Antione-Simon Le Page du Pratz's *History of Louisiana* "wherein the natural history sections are full of errors. . . ." For fauna identification Custis relied on Linnaeus's *Systema Naturae*, and, interestingly, Jefferson's own *Notes on the State of Virginia*.

As for transportation, Dunbar—using the experience gained in his own excursion—designed two twenty-five-foot-long flat-bottomed river vessels which drew only twenty inches of water when fully loaded. Measuring eight feet wide, both were mounted with "commodious Cabins" for the expedition's scientific and military leaders. These two craft, built in New Orleans, were later supplemented with five large pirogues, or dugout canoes, carved from cypress trees. "Although no information is available as to what firearms were carried by the party," wrote Flores, "probably they were a mixture of assorted Pennsylvania-Kentucky rifles and perhaps a few Model 1803 .54 caliber rifles. . . ."

But what of the Spanish? Their forces in east Texas were certainly poised to interfere with foreign expeditions. As noted above, early on Jefferson had begun working on the Spanish part of the puzzle. In the spring of 1805 the president wrote Louisiana Governor William

C. C. Claiborne asking him to secure a passport—safe passage—for the expedition from the former Spanish governor, the Marqués de Casa Calvo, who had stayed behind in New Orleans as a boundary commissioner. Claiborne explained that the purpose of the party was geographic, for, just as Jefferson had written, "we have to settle a boundary with Spain to the Westward, [and] they cannot expect us to go blindfold[ed] into the business." Casa Calvo, wrote historian Carl Newton Tyson, "was certain that the mission was designed to collect military information about the region and to agitate the natives against the Spaniards."

This was a period of strained relations between Spain and the United States. American incursions into the Louisiana Territory caused further friction over the boundary question because Spanish officials feared that the United States was expansionist in nature. The earlier Lewis and Clark Expedition, for example, had alarmed the commandant-general of the Internal Provinces of New Spain, Nemesio Salcedo. From his headquarters in Chihuahua he had three times ordered Spanish military forces to intercept and arrest the party. Of course none of these caught up with Lewis and Clark. Suspicious of U.S. designs in the Southwest, Salcedo later issued a proclamation banning all Americans from Texas, and positioned a blocking force upriver on the Red. In February of 1806 this garrison was forced to withdraw by a larger American force. Surprisingly, despite this contentious state of affairs, Casa Calvo consented to the passport, simultaneously notifying his superiors of the planned expedition. Salcedo exploded when he received word, ordering the "Governors of the Provinces adjacent to the United States . . . to Suspend the operations of any and all expeditions which may present themselves. . . ." Jefferson's "Grand Excursion" into the Southwest was about to enter a region claimed by both the United States and Spain.

Numbering twenty-four men, "The Exploring Expedition of Red River"—as Freeman and Custis styled their effort—departed from Fort Adams, on the Mississippi River, on April 19, 1806. "The plan," wrote historian Donald Jackson, "was to find the approximate source of the Red, supposedly in the country of the Pawnees, then to go on horseback to the 'top of the mountains' from which the river was thought to flow." The leaders of the expedition were instructed, by both Dunbar and Jefferson, to keep journals and to draw up scientific charts. Jefferson, of course, desired an accurate map of the Red River—this meant that the party would have to pause at every river bend to take sextant readings. To return, the expedition would float back down the Red River.

"In ascending a navigable river, whose banks are generally elevated considerably above the surface of the water," penned Freeman in his first entry, "the remarks of the survey will be confined to the width, depth, and course it pursues; and its rise during periods of inundation; the quality of the water, the vegetation on the banks ... as well as the animals and fish which art or accident may bring within [our] reach; together with the mineralogical and geological facts, which the abrasion of the waters furnish, confine the naturalist and chemist within very narrow bounds."

"The Red River," wrote Custis early on, "is at its mouth about a half mile wide and preserves that width for one mile and contracts to about a fourth of a mile and continues of that width as far as the mouth of the Black River, a distance of 30 miles from the Mississippi.—The water of [the] Red River is of a reddish brown colour [sic] caused by the suspension of an argillaceous [or clayey] marle of which the banks, in many places after passing Black River, seem to be almost entirely composed. From the colour [sic] is derived its name. For two or three miles this River is beautifully bordered with willow trees which extend back for half a mile where there is a second bank about 6 feet above the first." The adjective "beautiful," as used by Custis above, wrote Flores, "connotes not just a pleasing visual impression, but also potential agricultural fertility."

Fifty miles above the Black River the expedition arrived at the falls of the Red. "When we passed," penned Custis, "there was a fall of about four feet perpendicular & in the course of fifty yards, the extent of the falls, there was probably a fall of two feet more. The water was so shallow immediately above, that our boats . . . had to be unloaded & drawn over." Here, on the left bank, was the sprawling settlement Custis called "rapide Courthouse" (present-day Alexandria, Louisiana). Supposedly the site of a 1690 Spanish Franciscan mission, "Rapide Settlement"—as it was also called— prospered once the French erected a fort in the 1720s. The river's lush bottomlands offered excellent grazing and eventually became extensive fields of cotton. In 1806 the town's population was about 750.

"Twenty-three miles higher up the river than the falls," wrote Freeman, "on a bluff about 50 feet higher than . . . the water, is an Indian Village, called the Appalaches. . . . These Indians appear to be rapidly advancing towards civilization; they possess horses, cattle and hogs; dress better than Indians generally do, and seem to derive a considerable portion of their support from the cultivation of the earth." Natives of Florida, the Appalaches had relocated to the Red River. "Most of the Indians Freeman and Custis encountered," wrote Flores, "were immigrant Creeks moving west ahead of the Americans."

Above the Indian village, the river, wrote Freeman, "divides into two branches; that to the right is about one third of the whole width of the river, [and] retains the name of Red River, but is impassable, on account of the rafts of timber which are lodged in it. It separates from the other branch . . . called Old or Cane river . . . forming an island nearly sixty miles in length." Following the Cane River the expedition soon thereafter turned into another, more navigable branch named Little River which was seventy yards wide and twenty-four feet deep. "[T]he land on both banks is generally cultivated," wrote Freeman, "particularly the left bank, which presents a series of small plantations, each having one field in front. . . . The inhabitants are a mixture of French, Spanish, Indian, and Negro blood, the latter often predominating, and live in small cottages on the banks. . . ."

On May 19 the Freeman and Custis Expedition poled into Natchitoches (pronounced "Nack–a-tush"), 184 miles upriver from the Mississippi. "Founded in 1714," wrote Flores, "Natchitoches was the oldest continually occupied European site in the Louisiana Purchase" and had been "garrisoned by the United States in 1804." With a population of perhaps 600, the ramshackle river town was small—"meanly-built" according to Dr. John Sibley, the local U.S. Indian Agent. A physician fascinated by botany, geology, and Indian ethnology, Sibley had sent Jefferson a detailed description of the river below Natchitoches, as well as four pages of data entitled "Sibley's Acct. of the Indians." From his post in Natchitoches Sibley was urged, wrote Jackson, to "cultivate the friendship of the tribes in the event of a conflict with Spain." Somehow the good doctor also found time to investigate the local mineral deposits. "Doctor Sibley of this place," wrote Custis, "put into my hands an ore which he says is found in the greatest abundance on some of the branches of this river." Examining the small crystallized cubes, Custis classified them as "Iron Pyrites." This, according to Flores, is the earliest reference to the massive iron-ore beds that reach across east Texas and northern Louisiana.

The exploring expedition remained in Natchitoches until June 2. During the layover, Freeman procured two dozen barrels of flour, trade goods and trinkets for the Native Americans, and several guides and translators for the advance into the wilderness beyond. Additionally, a detachment of twenty soldiers led by Lieut. John Joseph DuForest was added "for the purpose of assisting the exploring party to ascend the river," penned Freeman, "and . . . to repel by force any opposition they might meet with." This number raised the expedition's total to forty-seven and occasioned the need to add four more pirogues to the tiny flotilla.

Freeman and Custis departed Natchitoches on June 2. Five days later the expedition arrived at what Freeman called "the highest white settlement [meaning the furthest upriver], which is a small plantation on the North side of the river, 45 miles above Natchitoches. . . . The

Cotton Wood Tree grows to a great size in this neighborhood; one standing in a cornfield, was found to be five feet in diameter and 141 and a half feet high."

It was in this neighborhood, too, that the party first encountered the downriver portions of the Great Raft, a virtually impenetrable mass of logs. "It consists of the trunks of large trees," penned Freeman, "lying in all directions, and damming up the river for its whole width, from the bottom, to about three feet higher than the surface of the water. The wood lies so compact that large bushes, weeds and grass cover the surface of the raft. . . . [T]he trees of which it is composed are Cotton Wood, Cypress, Red Cedar, &c. and they lie so close that the men could walk over it in any direction."

Blocking up the Red River for 100 miles, the Great Raft, wrote Flores, "was one of the amazing phenomena of natural North America. In terms of size and age, the gigantic logjam had no parallel on the rest of the continent's rivers." Thought to have originated around 1100 A.D., one theory claims that the Raft was formed when a powerful flood on the Mississippi River actually reversed the flow on the Red. Flores believed that the Red River "has always been inclined to block itself with drift debris. It is a shallow river . . . [and] flows through an alluvial, loamy country . . . with banks that are friable and cave readily. . . . Freshets thus toppled into the stream great numbers of living trees. . . ."

The expedition bypassed the Raft by detouring through the Great Swamp, a tedious water route that included interconnected lakes and bayous. "Being informed by M. Touline," wrote Freeman, "(a French gentleman born in the Caddo Nation . . .) that it was absolutely impractical to pass the great raft in boats of any kind; as neither Red nor White men had attempted it for 50 years before, and, that this was the only communication . . . we here left the river and entered the Bayou."

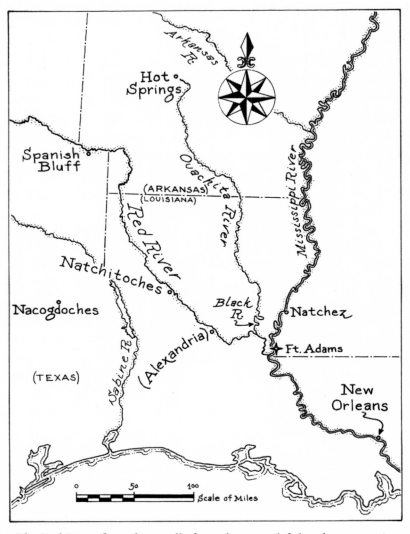

The Red River flows diagonally from the upper left-hand corner to its
confluence with the Mississippi just below Fort Adams.
(Map by the author.)

It was at this point, on June 8, that Freeman and Custis learned that the Spanish were making moves to intercept them. That afternoon, Sibley overtook the expedition to inform them of "the marching of Spanish Troops from Nacogdoches," (pronounced "Nack-a-doe-chis"), which was about seventy-five miles to their southwest. Nacogdoches was the east Texas headquarters of Capt. Don Francisco Viana, the adjutant inspector for Spanish forces in the Internal Provinces. An experienced soldier, Viana, on learning of the Americans on the Red, began gathering reinforcements—540 arrived by early June—and drilling his garrison. The Spanish were preparing for war.

Beyond the Great Raft lay a region inhabited by the Caddo Indians. On June 26 the expedition reached the village of the Alabama-Coushatta Indians, close allies of the Caddoes. Standing on the north side of the river, on a handsome bluff, this little village, wrote Freeman, "has been built within two or three years, and consists of 6 or 8 families of stragglers from the lower Creek Nation." After setting up camp nearby, the Americans were visited by the local chief. Freeman presented him with an American flag which "was hoisted on a pole in the middle of the square of the village, where it was kept constantly flying."

The chief of the Caddo Nation, Dehahuit, along with his young men and warriors arrived on July 1. Sitting in a semicircle, they were told through an interpreter "that France for certain consideration," wrote Custis, "had sold to the United States the whole country of Louisiana together with its inhabitants . . . and that henceforward the People of the United States would be their fathers & friends and would protect them & supply their wants." On hearing this Dehahuit expressed "great satisfaction." Afterwards, the soldiers were drawn up in single file and the Caddoes marched past them, shaking hands. During this ceremony the principal Caddo warrior announced "that he was glad to see his new brothers had the faces of *men*, and looked like men and warriors."

Unfortunately for the Americans, another band of warriors—this one unfriendly—was rapidly approaching. "The Caddoes . . . tell us," wrote Custis, "that the Spanish forces have retired . . . but it is generally believed to be a sham and that they intend to meet us on the River a little above this. This expedition seems to have thrown their whole Country into commotion."

The expedition left the Alabama-Coushatta village on July 11 and poled upriver, entering the Great Bend section where the Red—from the explorers' point of view—turns ninety degrees to the west over the course of fifty miles. "From the [Indian village] to where the [Little River] enters the red river, a distance of 162 miles," wrote Freeman, "the Valley of the Red river is one of the richest and most beautiful imaginable. It is from 6 to 10 miles in width, and . . . cannot be exceeded either in fertility or beauty, by any part of America, or perhaps the world. Through this valley, the Red River pursues a very winding course, in a bed varying from 200 to 250 yards in width, and between banks of from 15 to 20 feet high." On these banks stood groves of "Cotton Wood, Sycamore, Cypress, Black Gum, White and Black Oak, Hickory, Black Walnut, Pecan, Ash, Locust, and Red Cedar."

But time was quickly running out for "The Exploring Expedition of Red River." On July 26 Caddo runners arrived with the information that "Spanish troops upwards of 1,000 in number [had entered their village] . . . cut down the staff on which the American Flag was flying, and carried off the Flag with them." The Spanish also insulted their chief. But a few years earlier, Tripoli had declared war on the U.S. in a similar episode involving a flag. Called in the newspapers "a hostile demonstration of war," this incident later sparked a series of sharp diplomatic salvoes.

Three days later, on July 29, the Spaniards finally caught up with Freeman and Custis. Known today as Spanish Bluff, the site is 615 miles above the Mississippi River. All were quiet as the Spanish officers cantered toward Freeman and Captain Sparks. They "seemed to respect and fear," wrote Freeman, "the decision and arrangement made for their reception [and] during the conference, watched with anxiety the bank where the men were posted. . . . In this conference [Captain Viana] stated that his orders were not to suffer any body of armed troops to march through the territory of the Spanish Government; to stop the exploring party by force, and to fire on them if they persisted in ascending the river, before the limits of the territory were defined."

"I stated," explained Freeman, "that the object of my expedition was, to explore the river to its source, under the instructions of the President of the U.S. and I requested the Spanish commander to state in writing his objections to the progress of the party, and the authority upon which they were made." This Viana refused, and immediately asked if the Americans would turn back, and when. Noting the superiority of the Spanish force—and recognizing that the river's shallowness made further progress impracticable— Freeman replied that he would remain but one day, and turn back the day following. Within three weeks the weary explorers were back in Natchitoches on their way to Fort Adams.

Following his return, Freeman received a number of important government appointments. He surveyed the boundaries for the Chickasaw Treaty and performed census work in the Mississippi Territory. In the autumn of 1809—following Meriwether Lewis's apparent suicide at Grinder's Tavern on the Natchez Trace—it was Freeman who retrieved his fellow explorer's personal effects, including Lewis's journal, and took them to Virginia where he presented them to Thomas Jefferson. In 1811, Thomas Freeman became the nation's surveyor general. Thomas Freeman died on November 8, 1821 in Huntsville, Alabama.

After the expedition, Peter Custis completed his medical education, writing his thesis on "Bilious Fever in Albemarle County," then— apparently fed up with exploring—settled down to a medical practice in New Bern, North Carolina. He died there on May, 1, 1842.

For two hundred years the Freeman and Custis Expedition has been completely overshadowed by Lewis and Clark's fabled journey.

When history does remember "The Exploring Expedition of Red River," unfortunately, two facts predominate—it was checked by military force, and it was a failure. Freeman and Custis had failed to explore the entire river, failed to find its headwaters, and failed to evade the Spanish. Also in that regard, the termination of their effort put an end to Jefferson's dream of finding a southern water route to the Rockies. And the end result caused the president political embarrassment, for, as noted by Jackson, the decision to go ahead with the expedition "put in danger the lives of Americans pursuing an impossible goal."

Not all of the results of the Freeman and Custis Expedition, however, were negative. The Americans, for example, had won the friendship of the Alabama-Coushattas and the Caddoes. This factor led, in part, to America's future control of the Red River Valley. Also, the confrontation with the Spanish troops had been bloodless—luckily—and in the end failed to trigger a war between Spain and the U.S. Much useful information, too, had been gathered. Freeman and Humphreys's geographical field work was compiled and published in 1806—by Nicholas King—as the superb "Map of the Red River in Louisiana," which Flores called "a definitive chart of the lower 615 miles of the river. . . ." Freeman's journal entries, forwarded to Washington in two parts, were published in 1806 as *An Account Of The Red River, In Louisiana, Drawn Up From The Returns Of Messrs. Freeman & Custis* (of which today fewer than a dozen copies survive.) Custis—whom Flores called "the first American-trained naturalist to accompany an exploring expedition to the West"— later published his account of the lower river as "Observations relative to the Geography, Natural History, & etc., of the Country along the Red-River, in Louisiana" in Barton's *Philadelphia Medical and Physical Journal.* "As records of nineteenth-century scientific exploration," wrote Flores, "Freeman's journal and Custis's natural history catalogues provide valuable information on the Indian life and ecology of the Red River." President Jefferson, in his 1806 State of the Union Address, stated that the exploration had been pursued with "a zeal and prudence meriting entire approbation. . . ."

Edward Coles of Albemarle County (1786–1868).

IX

"THIS ENTERPRISE IS FOR THE YOUNG":
Edward Coles, Jefferson, & the "Peculiar Institution"

> *Let us hail the approach of that period when [the people of Illinois]*
> *shall be delivered from the trammels and shackles of territorial*
> *bondage.*
>
> *- Edward Coles, writing under the name "Agis," 1818*

It was a beautifully clear daybreak in April of 1819. Morning sunlight gleamed sharp across a boundless heaven of blue. The air was filled with the promising smells of spring. Close by, the picturesque banks of the Ohio were speckled with the colors of newfledged nature. On the broad water—one day's glide past Pittsburgh—drifted a pair of keelboats bound for a point below Louisville. Their cargo was the property of Mr. Edward Coles, late of Albemarle County, Virginia. Chattel slaves they were, over twenty men, women and children brought up in the Piedmont, now headed for an uncertain future in the new state of Illinois.

Coles had purposely hid his plans from his human property. They knew only that they were going into the Northwestern territory—into a land settled by both freemen and slaves. But this was the moment Edward Coles chose to instantaneously severe the manacles of inhuman bondage. He called to his Negroes across the lashed-together decks and announced, in as short a manner as possible, that they were no longer his. "You are all henceforth free," he said, "not slaves, but free—free as I am!—and free to continue on with me or to go ashore at your pleasure."

"The effect on them was electrical," he later wrote. At first they stared as if doubting the accuracy or even the reality of what they had heard. "Freedom, master? You're giving us our freedom?" Edward Coles simply nodded and smiled. Then, as the exorcising truth caught hold, "there came on a kind of hysterical, giggling laugh."

Care-worn stoic faces suddenly beamed, "with expression which no words could convey," he wrote, "and which no language can now describe." The long pent-up spirits were finally let loose, as Coles so wonderfully worded, "on the buoyant wings of liberty." Freedom!

Albemarle aristocrat Edward Coles, in one brave unselfish instant, had struck a personal blow against the practice of slavery. His continued struggle against the "blighting curse" placed him amongst the leaders of the anti-slavery forces in Illinois, and eventually carried him into the governor's mansion. It was a far-reaching example that his Albemarle neighbor, ex-president Thomas Jefferson, was unable to emulate.

Edward Coles had been born at "Enniscorthy"—in the Green Mountain area of Albemarle County—on December 15, 1786. He was the seventh son of John Coles II, who had served as a patriot colonel in the American Revolution. Visitors to the elder Coles's estate included Thomas Jefferson, James Madison, James Monroe, and Patrick Henry. "Enniscorthy" was a plantation of almost 5,000 acres tilled by bondsmen. Edward, therefore, grew up as a vested participant in the degrading enslavement of his fellow man.

Young Coles was tutored privately and attended both Hampden-Sydney and the College of William and Mary. His formal education was cut short, however, by a severe leg fracture. Among his many classmates were Winfield Scott, hero of the War of 1812 and the Mexican War, and John Tyler, tenth president of the United States.

It was in college that Coles first seriously considered the question of slavery. "He read everything on the subject that came his way," wrote biographer E. B. Washburne, "and listened to lectures on the rights of man." Did one man have the moral right to hold another man as his property? What obligations did the slave owners have for holding virtually an entire race of humans in bondage? And, if all the slaves were freed, would they be capable of fending for themselves?

Could they govern themselves? These were the questions and issues that swirled through the fertile brain of planter's son Edward Coles.

The more he pondered the more obvious became the answer. It was impossible to accommodate the crystalline language of the Declaration of Independence with a society which held human beings in perpetual servitude. "I could not reconcile it to my conscience . . . to participate in slavery"; he wrote, "and being unable to screen myself under such a shelter, from the peltings and upbraidings of my own conscience, and the just censure, as I conceived, of heaven and earth, I could not consent to hold as property what I had no right to, and which was not and could not be property according to my understanding of the rights and duties of man—and therefore I determined that I would not and could not hold my fellow man as a slave." He resolved also, wrote Washburne, not to live in "a State which upheld the institution of slavery."

These were noble sentiments surely, but they were perhaps best left unspoken among most of the Piedmont elites of the early nineteenth century. Their agrarian aristocracy was based, of course, on the amount of property owned—and that property included other humans. By the time Edward Coles reached his majority, slavery had existed in Virginia for almost two hundred years. Bondsmen, as well as white indentured servants, had been brought upstream into the Old Dominion's foothills during their earliest days of settlement. The Albemarle census figures of 1800 show 16,439 residents, of which number 7,436 were slaves (and only 207 were free blacks). Ten years later blacks slightly outnumbered whites in Coles's native county (and the number of freedmen remained proportionately tiny). "How [the slaves] fared day to day is pretty much a matter of conjecture," wrote historian John Hammond Moore, "but we can assume, human nature being what it is, that their existence was tedious and humdrum . . . and subject to the caprice of the head of the family they served. . . ." Economic conditions notwithstanding, slavery was thriving in the shadows of the Blue Ridge Mountains.

As a Piedmont Virginian Edward Coles was not alone in questioning what historian Kenneth M. Stampp termed "the peculiar institution." Thomas Jefferson, in his 1774 pamphlet entitled *A Summary View of the Rights of British America*, had vigorously attacked the trafficking of human beings and had declared the abolition of slavery, "the great object of desire in these colonies." Jefferson had also written about the corrupting effects of the institution on slaveholding families like the one residing at "Enniscorthy." "The whole commerce between master and slave is a perpetual exercise of the most boisterous passions, the most unremitting despotism on the one part, and degrading submissions on the other," wrote Jefferson in 1781. "Our children see this, and learn to imitate it; for man is an imitative animal." Edward Coles, however, would live to set a shining example to the contrary.

When John Coles II died in 1808, Edward and his brothers inherited the patriarch's property and way of life. So, at the age of twenty-two Edward Coles found himself the proprietor of lands—including a plantation on the Rockfish River—and slaves. He immediately began considering the possibility of manumitting his slaves (many of whom were possibly his half brothers and half sisters). But the free blacks young Coles had seen in the slave state of Virginia led miserable, poverty-stricken lives. And, in the early years of the nineteenth century, their prospects seemed to be diminishing.

Several other of young Coles's prominent neighbors in the Piedmont, including James Madison and John Hartwell Cocke, had struggled with the vexing problem of slavery during the revolutionary period and the twenty-five years since. Many had believed that general manumission must certainly come soon, thanks in part to their association with, what Robert McColley called, "the liberal vanguard of their times." The General Assembly of Virginia, however, as a collective body constructed legal barricades against these dispositions. An act of December, 1793, for example, made it a crime for anyone to import a free Negro into Virginia. The act of 1798 fined slave owners who licensed their bondsmen "to vend any goods, wares, or merchandise." But the worse blow against emancipation came in January of 1806. That month the legislature passed a law that newly freed slaves, who remained in the Commonwealth more than twelve months thereafter, "shall forfeit all such right, and may be apprehended and sold by the overseers of the poor of any county or corporation in which he or she shall be found."

In reaction various schemes were set forth to relocate freed blacks in the West Indies and Africa. Colonization, or re-colonization, became a familiar abolitionist solution to "the great political and moral evil," as Jefferson called it. Edward Coles perhaps first encountered the concept in Jefferson's *Notes on the State of Virginia*, written in 1781. In it the author of the Declaration laid out an intricate plan for gradual emancipation and removal. It had been part of a bill to "emancipate all slaves born after passing the act." The young slaves, he wrote, "should continue with their parents to a certain age, then be brought up, at the public expence [sic], to tillage, arts or sciences, according to their geniusses [sic], till the females should be eighteen, and the males twenty-one years of age, *when they should be colonized to such place as the circumstances . . . should render most proper . . .* [emphasis added]." The labor force thus lost to Virginia, reasoned Jefferson, could be replaced with a like number of imported whites. The bill, unfortunately, was never placed before the Virginia legislature. Edward Coles latched onto the idea of colonization, but his plans involved the lands in the Northwest. "Slowly the idea of transporting [his slaves] to free soil took form," wrote Vera Via, "and grew into a resolution."

In 1809 Edward Coles became the private secretary of newly elected president James Madison. Influential Piedmont connections had greatly benefited the young scion. Coles was related to Madison's wife Dolley, but he had also worked briefly as secretary for outgoing president Thomas Jefferson. Jefferson, in a March 5, 1809 letter to General John Armstrong, referred to his ex-secretary as "my wealthy neighbor at Monticello, and worthy of all confidence."

Edward Coles worked in the Federal Capital as President Madison's secretary for six years. "His great intelligence and his suavity of manner," wrote Washburne, "made him very useful to the President and very popular generally." Coles quickly acquired much knowledge of public affairs and public men. And, through his acquaintances in Washington, he was able to determine where best to settle in the public lands being opened up out west.

It was while he was still Mr. Madison's secretary that Edward Coles opened a correspondence with the "Sage of Monticello" on the subject of slavery. Jefferson, he knew, harbored similar views against the "peculiar institution" and also favored other doctrines that varied with the prevailing sentiments in Virginia. But many of their opinions on slavery and the black race in general differed greatly. Jefferson, of course, believed colonization was a possible solution, but he did not believe, for example, that the two races could live in harmony. In *Notes on the State of Virginia* he had written: "Deep rooted prejudices entertained by the whites, ten thousand recollections, by the blacks, of the injuries they have sustained; new provocations; the real distinctions which nature has made; and many other circumstances, will divide us into parties, *and produce convulsions which will probably never end but in the extermination of the one or the other race* [emphasis added]."

Also Jefferson, in classic patriarchal fashion, had classified some of the black racial distinctions he considered substandard. They included color, hair, figure, "want of forethought," inferior reasoning, an existence "more of sensation than reflection," their "disposition to sleep," and their "dull, tasteless" imagination. It's interesting to wonder how a man of Thomas Jefferson's capacity failed to grasp that the very differences he listed—aside from the subjective matter of beauty, of course—were the direct circumstances of the horrible institution he himself detested.

Coles, on the other hand, believed the races could co-exist. And he did not believe that blacks were inferior, nor that they would have any problems participating in the Republic. He wrote, for example, "that the descendants of Africa were competent to take care of and govern themselves, and enjoy all the blessings of liberty, and all the other birthrights of man. . . ." He was extremely confident of the bondsmen's ability, after obtaining freedom, to learn and prosper.

With these issues in mind twenty-seven year old Edward Coles wrote to Jefferson at Monticello on July 31, 1814:

> Dear Sir: I never took up my pen with more hesitation, or felt more embarrassment than I now do in addressing you on the subject of this letter. . . . My object is to entreat and beseech you to exert your knowledge and influence in devising and getting into operation some plan for the gradual emancipation of slavery [in Virginia]. . . . And it is a duty, as I conceive, that devolves particularly on you, from your known philosophy and enlarged view of subjects, and from the principles you have professed and practiced. . . . In the calm of this retirement you might . . . put into complete practice those hallowed principles contained in that renowned Declaration. . . . If [however] your attempt should now fail to rectify this unfortunate evil . . . at some future day when your memory will be consecrated by a grateful posterity, what irresistible influence will the opinions and writings of Thomas Jefferson have in all questions connected with the rights of man. . . .

> [From] the time I was capable of reflecting on . . . the rights appertaining to man, I have not only been principled against slavery, but have had feelings so repugnant to it as to decide to leave my native State, and with it all my friends and relations. . . . I am, my dear Sir, your very sincere and devoted friend,

> - Edward Coles

The seventy-year-old ex-president replied within a month. Jefferson's response contained, wrote Washburne, "the most pronounced views on the question of slavery that had ever been put forth by so distinguished a man residing in a slaveholding community." It was dated August 25, 1814:

> Dear Sir: Your favor of July 31 was duly received, and was read with peculiar pleasure; the sentiments breathed through the whole do honor to both the head and heart of the writer. [My opinions] on the subject of the slavery of negroes have long since been in possession of the public [as in *Notes on the State of Virginia*]. . . . The love of justice and the love of country plead equally the cause of these people, and it is a mortal reproach to us that they should have pleaded it so long in vain. . . . I have considered the general silence which prevails on this subject as indicating an apathy unfavorable to every hope, yet emancipation is advancing in the march of time. . . .
>
> I am sensible of the partialities with which you have looked towards me as the person who should undertake this salutary but arduous work; but this, my dear Sir, is like bidding old Priam to buckle [on] the armor of Hector. . . . No, I have overlived the generation with which mutual labors and perils begat mutual confidence and influence. This enterprise is for the young, for those who can follow it up and bear it through to its consummation. It shall have all my prayers, and these are the only weapons of an old man. But in the meantime, are you right in abandoning this property, and your country with it? I think not. . . . I assure you of my great friendship and respect.
>
> - Thomas Jefferson

Edward Coles read his neighbor's missive with the eager anticipations of youth. It was succinct and poignant, but it was also disappointing. In his reply from Washington, dated September 26, Coles rejected Jefferson's admonition against leaving Virginia. Remaining, and continuing to hold other humans in bondage, he believed, would accomplish nothing. He was not himself, "capable of being instrumental in bringing about a liberation" in Virginia, he wrote, and so had determined to carry his slaves, "to the country northwest of the river Ohio." To Jefferson's excuse of old age he responded that "Doctor [Benjamin] Franklin, to whom, by the way Pennsylvania owes her early riddance of the evils of slavery, was as actively and as usefully employed on as arduous duties after he had past your age as he had ever been at any period of his life." Coles ended this letter by, "apologizing for having given you so much trouble on this subject. . . ."

The following year Edward Coles made the first of two horse-and-buggy trips into the West in search of land to settle. He visited Ohio, Indiana, Missouri, Mississippi and Louisiana. In the Territory of Illinois he rode from Shawneetown to St. Louis. His great project was delayed, however, when President Madison sent him to Russia on diplomatic business. While in Europe he traveled extensively through Germany, France, and England.

During the summer of 1818 Edward Coles returned to investigate the wild western country of Illinois. With him he carried a letter of introduction from the president of the United States to Gov. Ninian Edwards. In it James Monroe described Coles as a man of "great industry and fidelity, and [who] is generally loved by those who know him best." "Should he settle with you," continued the Virginia president, "you will find him a very useful acquisition— and I understand that is not an improbable event." For settlement Coles chose part of the fertile prairie just east of the Mississippi River near Edwardsville.

Coles work against slavery in Illinois began during his second tour of discovery. Illinois was no stranger to the horrible practice. The Illinois Indians, surprisingly enough, had often held captured Pawnees as slaves and had presented one to French explorers Louis Jolliet and Jacques Marquette in 1673. Philippe Renault brought 500 black slaves into Illinois in 1719. The "peculiar institution" continued in Illinois and the opposing forces struggled over the issue when the territory became a state. Edward Coles used whatever influence he had to benefit the anti-slavery camp. During his 1818 trip Coles spent time at Kaskaskia, then the seat of government, in order to help prevent, wrote Washburne, "any recognition of slavery in the constitution of the State which he desired to make his home."

Edward Coles's great experiment came to fruition in the spring of 1819. He sold his lands in Albemarle and sent his slaves to the northwest in covered wagons under the care of one of their own, Ralph Crawford. At Brownsville, Pennsylvania Coles met up with his little caravan and transferred them onto keelboats for the ride down the Ohio River. From there he sent back a letter to his brother John in Virginia. Ralph Crawford, he wrote proudly, had "conducted the party with as much judgment and economy as anyone, even of the glorious Saxon race, could have done."

Following the wishes of his family, Coles kept his wonderful plans a complete secret until they were floating safely along the beautiful Ohio. As the shock of total freedom swept across the small group Ralph Crawford stepped forward. They should not be freed, he argued, until they had paid for their passage. And they should stay together until their master had improved his lands and they had, wrote Coles, "gotten me well fixed in that new country."

"No," answered Coles. "As a reward for their past services, [and] as a stimulant to their future exertions," he was freeing them unconditionally and was giving each head of household 160 acres in Illinois. And he hoped they would do well, he later wrote, "not only for their own sakes, but for the sake of the black race held in bondage; many of whom were thus held, because their masters believed they were incompetent to take care of themselves, and that liberty would be to them a curse rather than a blessing." To these immortal ends he then gave each a general certificate of freedom.

In Illinois they all began anew, therefore, working together as equals on what Edward Coles called his Prairie Land Farm. He had emancipated them, but it was the ownership of property that made freedom a reality. Ralph Crawford died soon after reaching Illinois, unfortunately, but his brother Robert prospered and became a founder of the Black Methodist Church of Illinois.

In 1819 Edward Coles was made registrar of land in Edwardsville. This new position was one of prominence—he used it to continue the struggle against human bondage. Shortly thereafter, when slaveholding forces were fighting for a convention to declare Illinois a slave state, Coles led the opposition. As "Agis" he wrote: "I would rather see our rich meadows and fertile woodlands inhabited alone by the wild beasts and birds of the air, than they should ever echo the sound of the slave driver's scourge." He was elected governor in 1822 by a small margin, and re-elected in 1824. After losing a bid for Congress, Edward Coles quit his adopted state and retired to Philadelphia. There he married Sallie Logan Roberts in 1832, and there was born his only son, Roberts.

Irony calls to us from the past in many forms and guises. Roberts Coles defiantly returned to his father's native state and took up the sword in defense of Virginia and her "peculiar institution." He was put in command of a company from Albemarle. Captain Roberts Coles was killed at the Battle of Roanoke Island on February 8, 1862 while leading Co. I of the 46th Virginia Infantry, the "Green Mountain Greys." His commanding officer described him as "a gallant soldier."

A correspondent for *The New York Times*, in walking over the battlefield, "came across the body of a well-dressed officer lying with face upturned and eyes partially closed." On inquiring the newspaper man was told the dead man's identity and that his parents "lived in Philadelphia near the intersection of Spruce and 13th Streets." Touched, the writer snipped a lock of Roberts's hair to mail home to his parents.

Albemarle native Edward Coles died in 1868. He had lived according to his own powerful principles and had battled fervently, and successfully, against the greatest evil then plaguing our young nation. We can only hope that his virtuous soul found rest.

*The Marquis de Lafayette (1757–1834)
as a young American general.*

X

"THE LIVELY SENTIMENTS OF JOY":

The Marquis de Lafayette's 1824 Visit

"In moral sublimity there is nothing like it in the history of man. Triumphs have been awarded and instituted by law, but here is an instance of a private individual of foreign birth, enjoying a splendid triumph throughout a whole nation . . . awarded to him by the spontaneously feelings of a grateful people."
- Anonymous Newspaper Reporter, 1824

As the grand procession descended the hill across from the Rivanna River town of Milton the lead cavalry horses noisily began splashing into the ford. Startled birds flapped into the air and fluttered to the south over Monticello. Work was temporarily halted in Milton as the inhabitants rushed to the right bank. It was the early afternoon of November 4, 1824.

Behind the trim cavalry detachment rode the gaudily dressed Committee of Arrangements. Their high hats and black tails bobbed about as their mounts high-stepped through the chilly water. When the well-appointed four-horse landau eased across the Rivanna—closely followed by a motley array of mounted citizens—the crowd on the south shore got its first glimpse of the "hero of two worlds" riding inside. Here, just as everywhere else along his route, the spectators shouted greetings to this old friend of the young Republic. "Welcome Lafayette!" they cheered, "Welcome back!" Inside the Marquis marveled at the landscape that brought back so many pleasant memories.

Several miles after passing the river the long procession slowly ascended Monticello Mountain. A loud bugle sounded when the leading cavalrymen broke through the ring of trees north of the house. As the final notes echoed over the Southwest Mountains and nearby Charlottesville, the large crowd that had assembled at an early hour formed along the yard's western margin. The saber-wielding troopers jangled onto the yard and ranged themselves on the opposite side. All eyes followed the general's carriage as it wheeled to a halt at the gate leading to Monticello's east portico. Solemn quiet reigned as Lafayette alit. From the base of the portico steps a feeble Thomas Jefferson—enveloped in a long coat against the chill—tottered forward to greet Lafayette, and as the two old revolutionaries drew near emotions overcame them both. Thirty-five years had passed since they had last seen each other. To the obvious delight of the crowd they embraced over and over. "God bless you general," uttered the author of the Declaration of Independence. "Bless you my dear Jefferson," came the reply.

Marie-Joseph-Paul-Yves-Roch Gilbert du Motier, Marquis de Lafayette had been born on September 6, 1757 at Chateau Chavaniac in central France, seventy-five miles southwest of Lyons. His was an ancient noble family—one of significant means. Lafayette's father, a colonel of French grenadiers, was killed fighting the British at the 1759 battle of Minden. "Lafayette's widowed mother," penned Rick Bromer, "was nineteen years old and a beauty." Raised at the ancestral estate by his paternal grandmother—who "in love with the myths of chivalry," according to Bromer, "told her grandson endless tales of knights-errant, tournaments, and courtly love"—Lafayette had already inherited a huge fortune by the time of his 1774 marriage to Adrienne de Noailles, the daughter of the powerful duc d'Ayen. With wealth and family influence under his belt, as well as a commission in the famous Black Musketeers, the Marquis de Lafayette seemed destined to ride into family legend alongside the gallant ancestors who had drawn their broadswords in the Crusades and sworn allegiance to Joan of Arc.

In 1776, events an ocean away forever altered Lafayette's life. When the upstart British colonies defied the authority of the crown with their Declaration of Independence the nineteen-year-old Marquis determined to lend his sword to the American cause. He purchased his own vessel in April of 1777 and, without official permission, sailed for the embattled colonies. Ideologically,

Lafayette's views were perfectly matched with the colonial fight for independence. "The welfare of America," he wrote his family after landing in South Carolina, "is intimately connected with the happiness of all mankind."

In July of 1777 Lafayette was accepted by Congress as an unpaid volunteer on the staff of Gen. George Washington. The warm relationship that developed between these two is well-known. In early December of the same year Lafayette obtained his own command, a division of Virginians, and the rank of major general. At age twenty the Marquis de Lafayette was the youngest general in the American forces. He spent part of the shivering winter of 1777–78 with the troops at Valley Forge and the following year performed admirably in independent command on a number of occasions.

In 1779 the Marquis returned to France. French troops had already taken part in the war, but in Paris Lafayette used his connections to help Benjamin Franklin plead for more assistance. On April 26, 1780 Lafayette landed in Boston with advance news of the mobilization of a second—larger—French expeditionary army to the colonies. Fifty-five hundred French infantrymen, five ships of the line, and five frigates were on their way under the able Comte de Rochambeau.

Washington was eager for the added French troops but was also glad to have his enthusiastic young protégé back with the army. Lafayette was dispatched to Virginia where British General Lord Cornwallis—with over 7,000 troops—was threatening to overrun the most populous state. It was in Virginia, in fact, that the Marquis de Lafayette made his greatest contribution to the American war effort. With a force of approximately 800 Continentals—bolstered at times with militia detachments—the young major general was able to spar with Cornwallis and at the same time protect many of the state's war resources. Lafayette skirmished with the British and constantly harassed their flanks but skillfully avoided fighting a set-piece battle that he simply could not win.

When the frustrated Cornwallis retreated to Yorktown Lafayette followed. The Marquis thus began the decisive entrapment that ended with the surrender of Cornwallis on October 19, 1781. "America is assured her independence," he wrote following the amazing victory, "mankind's cause is won and liberty is no longer homeless on earth."

At the close of this very successful military campaign Lafayette returned to the land of his birth. There he soon established his place in the forefront of French military and political circles. He was awarded the rank of major general and became a member of the Assembly of Notables. Lafayette was elected as a representative of the nobility to the Estates General in 1789. When that body was converted into a National Assembly he introduced his "Declaration of the Rights of Man and of the Citizen." A revised version was adopted shortly thereafter. On July 15, 1789—the day after the storming of the Bastille—Lafayette was elected commander of the Paris National Guard. In that position he maintained power and influence through the grim years of the French Revolution. When the new constitution was adopted in October of 1791, Lafayette—his popularity on the wane due to an incident in which his soldiers shot fifty demonstrators—resigned from the guard.

The Marquis de Lafayette was in command of an army at Metz—on the frontier—when France declared war on Austria in April of 1792. Very vocal in his support of the king, Lafayette was impeached by the National Assembly when Louis XVI was deposed three months later. Fearing the guillotine he defected to the Austrians, who imprisoned him until 1797. Lafayette returned to France two years later when Napoleon came to power. World weary at the age of forty-three, Lafayette settled into the rolling farmland at Chateau La Grange, outside of Paris.

During Napoleon's reign the Marquis remained a gentleman farmer, even though the emperor often tempted him with honors and offices. As an elected member of the Chamber of Deputies

(1814–24), Lafayette pushed for the abdication of Napoleon after the disastrous defeat at Waterloo. During his nine more years as a member of the Chamber he supported numerous revolutions, in Latin America as well as in Europe, even though it cost him dearly in French political circles.

This then was the sixty-seven-year-old Marquis de Lafayette who stepped from the carriage at Monticello in November of 1824. He had spent a lifetime in the fight for freedom and had played a grand role in two of the most momentous revolutions of his lifetime.

Lafayette's "Triumphal Tour" of the United States of America had come about thanks to a very special invitation. In March of 1824 the Marquis received a letter from President James Monroe urging him to cross the Atlantic. "The whole nation," wrote the fourth Virginia president, "ardently desire[s] to see you again among them." Attached was the following unanimously passed joint resolution of Congress:

> *"Resolved, by the Senate and House of Representatives of the United States of America in Congress Assembled,* That the President be requested to communicate to [Lafayette] the assurances of grateful and affectionate attachment still cherished for him by the Government and people of the United States.
>
> *And be it further resolved,* That, whenever the President shall be informed of the time when the Marquis may be ready to embark, that a national ship (with suitable accommodations) be employed to bring him to the United States."

Lafayette was moved by the invitation and graciously accepted, although he turned down the use of an American warship. Enthusiasm ran high as America contemplated on how best to receive its "adopted son." Every town and hamlet passed special resolutions in preparation for his reception. And no small amount of thought was given to his financial arrangements. "It is understood that he will be at no expense in the cities," announced the Washington, D.C. *National Journal* of August 5, 1824, "He ought to be at no expense anywhere. It is hoped that he will not be permitted to expend one cent in the United States. . . . "

The Marquis de Lafayette arrived in New York on Sunday morning, August 15, 1824. The American merchantman *Cadmus* had transported him from the French port of Le Havre. The Marquis was accompanied by his son George—named for General Washington—his secretary Auguste Levasseur and a personal valet named Bastien. The city of New York exploded in celebration. From New York the Marquis's busy itinerary took him to Providence, Boston, Portsmouth, back to New York, Albany, New York again, Philadelphia, Wilmington, Baltimore, and Washington. Receptions, celebrations, and special dinners were held at every town and stopover along the way. From Washington the Marquis descended the Potomac River to Yorktown, Virginia. A special commemoration was held at the historic battlefield forty-three years to the day after the British surrender. From Yorktown Lafayette traveled up the peninsula to Richmond. The general enjoyed his reception in Virginia's capital but he was eager to see an old friend who resided seventy miles to the west, just outside of Charlottesville.

As Lafayette's carriage approached the Southwest Mountains near Albemarle County on November 4 he was greeted by a large collection of well-dressed dignitaries and militiamen. A resplendent troop of the Albemarle Lafayette Guards under a Captain Craven drew their sabers in salute then rent the cool air with three loud, enthusiastic shouts of "Welcome Lafayette!" When the carriage halted in the roadway they formed around it in hollow square. An impressive welcome speech was delivered by William Cabell Rives of the Committee of Arrangements.

"We are come hither, in the name of the people of Albemarle," stated Rives, as recorded by Charles Downing for the Richmond *Enquirer*, "to meet you, at the *threshold* of our county, with a cordial and affectionate welcome, and to assure you of the lively sentiments of joy, with which your arrival amongst us is anticipated by every heart. In common with our fellow citizens throughout the United States, we cherish the most grateful recollection of the generous and devoted zeal, which, in the darkest aspect of our revolutionary fortunes, enlisted you in the support of our cause, and which, at the sacrifice of every present enjoyment and at the hazard of all your future prospects, retained you in it, 'till, by your aid it was crowned with the most glorious success. It was not the spirit of chivalry, however magnanimous, nor yet the love of fame, however honorable, which impelled you to this enterprise of noble daring. The history of your life bears witness that you were animated by the love of liberty alone. . . .

To your care was entrusted by the confidence of Washington . . . the defense of Virginia against the legions of an invading foe; and so happily did you prove yourself worthy of his choice, that . . . you kept him perpetually in check, and extended the shield of protection over every part of our territory. . . .

We are proud, General, exceedingly proud, of this opportunity of testifying to you, in person, the sentiments of gratitude, veneration and affection. . . . "

Lafayette listened quietly then responded warmly in heavily accented English that, nonetheless, surprised many of the attendees. (These formalities, after all, had become a daily experience for our nation's guest.) "I am happy to recognize the friendly partiality in my behalf . . . " concluded Lafayette, and "present to you and the citizens of Albemarle, the acknowledgments of a grateful heart, whose old devotion to this country, delights in their actual tranquility and happiness." The speechifying and cheering done the Marquis was escorted to Mrs. Boyd's Tavern where an elaborate layout of refreshments awaited.

At 12 o'clock a beautifully furnished carriage, sent by Thomas Jefferson, arrived to carry Lafayette to Monticello. It was drawn by four tall greys. A separate carriage was provided for his traveling companions, while a "neat" wagon transported their baggage. With the cavalrymen out front, the procession departed the tavern for the trip to Monticello. The route was lined with citizens straining to catch sight of the hero of the American Revolution. Many grizzled veterans of that struggle, then in their sixties through eighties, stepped to the highway's edge and saluted as Lafayette's coach rolled past. "Nothing could surpass in beauty and grandeur," reported the Fredericksburg *Virginia Herald* of November 15, "the march of a long and animated procession, through a mountain's meanders. . . ."

Jefferson's welcome at Monticello was emotionally draining for both men. Lafayette was shaken at the appearance of his friend and fellow revolutionary. Jefferson was eighty-one years old and had less than two years left to live. An observer described the Marquis as a tall man of strong features. Even though dressed plainly, his bearing clearly identified him as a man of dignity and strong convictions. As the cheering died down Jefferson and Lafayette retreated to the warmth of Monticello's library. There was much to talk about. Since they had last met Thomas Jefferson had served in America's highest office. Jefferson, no doubt, required a detailed recounting of the tumultuous French Revolution.

At 10 o'clock the next morning—it was Friday, November 5— the Committee of Arrangements and the Lafayette Guards returned to Monticello to escort the Marquis to nearby Charlottesville. In the landau along with Lafayette rode Jefferson and James Madison, who in 1817 had completed two terms as fourth president of the United States. At the Central Hotel in town Lafayette was cheered by a crowd of hundreds. Dozens of excited citizens leaned out of second-story windows waving handkerchiefs and small American flags.

"The crowd was great," noted the Fredericksburg *Herald*, "and there seemed but one feeling in the living mass—to see, to hear, to touch him. The General wore a pleased and smiling countenance. He was gratified at the glow of feeling—it was not constrained in respect to rank, to power—it was love—it was deep and grateful affection; it was the brazen memory of his services, and sacrifices for us that swelled the hearts and glistened in the eyes of the people." On the hotel steps he was formally greeted and replied "in handsome manner." Inside the Marquis was taken to a large room specially prepared for his reception. He was, according to Downing "introduced to everyone who desired it."

The next stop for the procession was one mile west of Charlottesville. The order of march, according to Downing, was as follows: "Chief Marshall, with two aids; President of the day; The General, Mr. Jefferson and Mr. Madison in a landau drawn by four greys; General's son and suits—Carriage with two cream colored horses; Visitors of the University of Virginia, in a carriage; Standing Committee; Magistrates; Cavalry; Junior Volunteers; Citizens on Horseback; [and] Citizens on foot." West Main Street that day was packed with cheering onlookers, including Robert Scott (1803–1899), whose family, wrote historian Lucia Stanton, "provided music for the festivities—some apparently at Monticello—in honor of Charlottesville's celebrated visitor." Years later Scott also recalled that the landau carriage in which rode Lafayette had been built by his uncles Joe Fossett and John Hemings—two of Jefferson's most talented slaves.

The long parade "moved slowly to the University," wrote Downing, "nothing could be more orderly performed: each man . . . seemed to have been drilled to his duty. The Lafayette Guards were quick and expert in their evolutions—the citizens orderly and decorous." Jefferson must have smiled proudly as the majestic University buildings came within sight. The Marquis and the two former presidents alighted on the southern end of the grounds and walked up the lawn to the Rotunda. The cavalrymen and dignitaries followed suit.

The lawn presented a curious sight that day. Arranged on the tops of the terraces were a thousand "daughters of the mountains" waving white handkerchiefs. Below, civilians crowded the covered walkways. Though yet to be completed the Rotunda was proudly flying three flags. The largest, in the center, carried the words "Welcome our Country's Guest."

From the steps of the Rotunda he was addressed in glowing terms by William Gordon, Esq. "Whilst with spontaneous gratitude," expounded Gordon, "millions of free men, resound to Heaven, the praise of liberty and Lafayette. The citizens of Virginia, hail with peculiar enthusiasm, your arrival at this spot. . . . For yourself, General, we sincerely pray, that a life which has been gloriously directed to the service and happiness of mankind, whose morning beam lighted the darkness of our fortunes, may be very long protracted. . . . " Lafayette, in his reply, was no less eloquent. "I am happy, sir, to receive the kind welcome of the citizens of Albemarle," he said, "and this day receive it under the beautiful pantheon of this rising University."

From the south portico of the Rotunda the Marquis retired to an apartment set aside for him in one of the adjacent pavilions. Shortly thereafter, escorted by the two ex-presidents, Lafayette, wrote Downing, "walked on the terraces, among the ladies, to many of whom he was introduced, and with whom he shook hands in the most courteous, and graceful manner." It was there, according to Lafayette biographer Etienne Charavay, that a university official commented on the general's amazing ability with English. "And why would I not speak English?" Lafayette shot back. "I am an American, after all—just back from a long visit to Europe."

At three o'clock the Marquis was invited to a dinner in the dome room of the Rotunda. Seating for 400 individuals was arranged with tables in three concentric circles. Over Lafayette's place was hung an arch of living laurel, wrote Downing, "beautifully entwined around two columns that supported the gallery."

"The meats were excellent," noted the Fredericksburg *Herald*, "and each eye around us beamed contentment. It was contentment from the performance of the most sacred, the most grateful duty. It was the offering of liberty to him who had gratuitously aided to achieve it." After the meal, toasts and speeches were made all around. The first toast to Lafayette resounded, penned Downing, "with enthusiastic cheering—the lofty dome of the Rotunda re-echoed back the sound—it rolled in billowy volumes around the spacious Hall, and sunk in the deep stillness of enthusiasm." Other toasts came in quick succession—to "The Sages and Heroes of the Revolution" and "The President of the U. States [James Monroe]— In the first war, he shed his blood for us—he aided in the second to its glorious termination. . . ."

Then the guests drank to "Thomas Jefferson and the Declaration of Independence—Alike identified with the cause of liberty." And everyone turned to the ex-president, awaiting an appropriate reply. Jefferson, unable to read perhaps because of the emotions of the moment, handed his brief speech to V. W. Southall. "His deeds in the war of independence you have heard and read," had written the Sage of Monticello. "They are known to you and embalmed in your memories, and in the pages of faithful history. His deeds, in the peace which followed that war, are perhaps not know[n] to you, but I can attest them. When I was stationed in his country for the purpose of cementing its friendship with ours . . . this friend of both was my most powerful auxiliary and advocate. He made our cause his own, as in truth it was that of his native country also. His influence and connections there were great. . . . In truth, I only held the nail, he drove it.—Honor him then, as your benefactor in peace as well as in war." The Marquis was greatly moved by his friend's tribute and, getting up from his place at the head table, grasped Jefferson's hand and wept out loud. "Oh, there is something magic and contagious," wrote Downing, "in the tears of a great man . . . there is something awful in that power that breaks open to the deep fountains of the heart until they overflow."

James Madison stood following Jefferson's short speech. "To liberty," exclaimed the father of the Constitution, "which has virtue for its guest and gratitude for its feast." Forty more toasts followed. At six o'clock the Marquis, Jefferson, and Madison were escorted back to Monticello by Capt. Craven's Lafayette Guards.

Lafayette remained at Monticello through the weekend of November 13 and 14. Doubtless the old friends passed the week reliving the days of the revolution and the momentous epoch they had shared. Virginia, perhaps more than any other one state, had benefited from Lafayette's military skill. The old veteran beamed when he spoke of the Virginia troops he had commanded.

Lafayette's farewell on Monday, November 15 was no less emotional than his welcome. His carriage was escorted to Orange County by 100 troopers of the Albemarle Lafayette Guards. When the Marquis departed Virginia for points north, the Charlottesville *Central Gazette* wrote, "We never can cease to cherish the most heartfelt and grateful remembrance of this universal friend of man, of this efficient benefactor of America, and of the human race."

Pavilions of the University's West Lawn.
(Photo by the author.)

XI

THE "HOBBY" OF JEFFERSON'S OLD AGE:
The Founding of the University of Virginia

A lbemarle County had never seen the like. The dusty roadway leading west from the little town of Charlottesville was crowded with hundreds of eager onlookers. The noisy throng included shop-owners, slaves, and several tottering veterans of the American Revolution. That day—it was November 5, 1824—the old patriots had buttoned on their tattered jackets in honor of the general they had not seen in over forty years. When the cavalcade finally approached the old soldiers saluted. The civilians cheered.

Leading the parade—astride a large, prancing charger—rode the event's "chief marshal" accompanied by his aides. Behind them rolled the center of attention—a magnificent, jet-black landau—in which sat, according to the Charlottesville *Central Gazette*, "a hero of the revolution with two of its sages": the Marquis de Lafayette accompanied by ex-presidents Thomas Jefferson and James Madison. In the back of the carriage, Jefferson must have smiled proudly as his University of Virginia came suddenly into view. The "Sage of Monticello," of course, simply had to give Lafayette a tour of the project he fondly called the "hobby" of his old age.

Of Thomas Jefferson's many and varied accomplishments, he asked that only three be inscribed on his tombstone: his authorship of the Declaration of Independence and the Virginia Statute for Religious Freedom, and his fathering of the University of Virginia. These achievements perfectly represent three of the ideals he held most dear—personal freedom, religious freedom, and education. Since opening its doors in 1825, sixteen months before Jefferson's death, the University has become one of the South's most renown institutions of higher learning. Its modern status, however, disguises the pains taken in its inception. The founding of the University of Virginia was a process of many years, much sweat, and considerable debate.

Thomas Jefferson was a life-long proponent of public education. The strength of this conviction was rooted, no doubt, in the basic fact that education in Virginia, until the end of the 1700s, was a very special privilege. "It was for clergymen and gentlemen—distinct as elements," wrote U.Va. librarian John S. Patton, "while the sons of the common people, a term then in frequent use, were well enough employed in making tobacco." The American Revolution changed all that. The nation's yeomanry—the small farmers, the citizen-soldiers—had won the war, and with it their equal share in the nation's future. Following the conflict, it was obvious, wrote Patton, "that men whose fathers had worn buckskin or jeans would exercise in the government an influence in some measure proportioned to their numbers . . . and that enlightenment would be the one certain safeguard of the sacred things of liberty."

Jefferson, of course, had enumerated those "sacred things," those "inalienable rights"—"life, liberty, and the pursuit of happiness"—in the Declaration. "Education," he wrote in 1818, "engrafts a new man on the native stock, and turns what in his nature was vicious and perverse into qualities of virtue and social worth. . . . And it cannot but be, that each generation succeeding to the knowledge acquired by all those that preceded it, adding it to their acquisitions and discoveries . . . must advance the knowledge and well-being of mankind, not infinitely, but indefinitely." As he related to George Ticknor: "Knowledge is power, knowledge is safety, knowledge is happiness."

The University of Virginia—the founding of which Jefferson called the hobby of his old age—went through several distinct phases in its development. Before opening its doors as the University in 1825, it had incarnations as Albemarle Academy and Central College. But to trace the institution's beginnings one must start almost fifty years before the first classes were held. In 1776, Thomas Jefferson—while chairing a committee of the Virginia General Assembly charged with restructuring the state's laws—developed a comprehensive plan for general education. "I accordingly prepared three bills for the Revisal," he wrote, "proposing three distinct grades of education, reaching all classes. 1. Elementary schools for all children generally, rich and poor. 2. Colleges for a middle degree of instruction, calculated for the common purposes of life, and such as would be desirable for all who were in easy circumstances. And 3d. an ultimate grade for teaching the sciences generally, & in their highest degree."

The proposal's preamble reveals Jefferson's reasoning on the value of public education. "Whereas, it appeareth," he noted, "that however certain forms of government are better calculated than others to protect individuals in the free exercise of their natural rights . . . yet experience hath shown that even under the best forms those entrusted with power . . . have perverted it into tyranny; and it is believed that the most effectual means of preventing this would be to illuminate, as far as practicable, the minds of the people at large . . . whence it becomes expedient, for promoting the public happiness, that those persons whom nature hath endowed with genius and virtue should be rendered, by liberal education, worthy to receive, and able to guard the sacred deposit of the rights and liberties of their fellow citizens, and that they should be called to the charge without regard to wealth, birth, or other accidental condition or circumstance." Though the plan was not adopted as proposed, the dream remained with him for the rest of his life.

The University of Virginia's first incarnation took shape in January of 1803. At that time Albemarle Academy, a secondary school for boys, was chartered by the Virginia legislature. Unfortunately, the records of further preliminary proceedings, if indeed there were any, have been lost. Albemarle Academy thus remained in a dormant state for the next eleven years, until the election of Mr. Jefferson to its Board of Trustees in March of 1814. At the next meeting, Peter Carr was chosen as president and the ex-president of the United States was made chairman of a committee tasked with recommending how to raise funds for construction and maintenance. "The committee reported within ten days;" wrote historian Herbert B. Adams, "subscriptions were recommended, [and] a lottery was proposed. . . ." A site-selection committee suggested in August that the academy be built in the vicinity of Charlottesville.

At about this time Jefferson wrote Peter Carr outlining his concepts for organizing Albemarle Academy. That was the initial intent, at least, but early on in the missive Jefferson suggested the possibility of expanding that institution into a college, with professional schools. Dated Monticello, September 7, 1814—and called by Adams "the most important document in the early history of the University of Virginia"—the letter was eventually printed in the Richmond *Enquirer* in order to popularize Jefferson's ideas. "I have long entertained the hope that this, our native State," he wrote, "would take up the subject of education, and make an establishment, either with or without incorporation into that of William and Mary, where every branch of science, deemed useful at this day, should be taught. . . ." Following his introductory remarks, Jefferson described three levels of schools (elementary, general, and professional, the last two grouped into "colleges"), and divided the citizenry into two classes: "laboring" and "learned." After noting that "every citizen . . . should receive an education proportioned to the condition and pursuits of his life," Jefferson remarked that the elementary schools—which would teach reading, writing, arithmetic, and geography—would suffice for the "laboring" class.

"At the discharging of the pupils from the elementary schools," he wrote, "the two classes separate—those destined for labor will engage in the business of agriculture, or enter into apprenticeships . . . [while] their companions, destined to the pursuits of science, will proceed to the college, which will consist, 1st of general schools; and, 2d, of professional schools." The science-minded students would begin learning the useful sciences in the general schools and then specialize in one particular branch in the professional schools.

The "useful sciences" were grouped by Jefferson into three departments: language, mathematics, and philosophy. The first included ancient and modern languages, grammar, belles-lettres, rhetoric, oratory, and history, "not as a kindred subject [to language]," he wrote, "but on a principle of economy, because both may be attained by the same course of reading. . . ." The mathematics department would teach pure mathematics, physico-mathematics, physics, chemistry, mineralogy, botany, zoology, anatomy, and the theory of medicine, while the philosophy department would feature ideology, ethics, government, political economy, and the law of nature and nations.

The professional schools Jefferson envisioned resembled today's universities: the students in these would be specializing with a definite purpose—a career—in mind. "In these professional schools," he wrote, "each science is to be taught in the highest degree it has yet attained." To these institutions would come, he prophesized, "the lawyer to the school of law . . . the physician to those of the practice of medicine, materia medica, pharmacy, and surgery . . . the agricultor to that of rural economy; [and] the gentleman, the architect, the pleasure gardener, painter, and musician, to the school of fine arts."

Jefferson even foresaw the need for technical education. To his separate school of "technical philosophy"—where the lectures would be held in the evenings—would come, among others, the mariner, carpenter, shipwright, mechanic, metallurgist, painter, soap-maker, tanner, and glass-maker. "Military exercises," wrote Adams, "were to be required on certain days throughout the course for all grades of students. Thus the features of military schools, technological institutes, and modern agricultural colleges were associated with the higher education in a people's university, as conceived by Thomas Jefferson."

On receiving the detailed letter, Peter Carr quickly realized that if the Albemarle Academy Board of Trustees had simply wanted to establish a grammar school in Charlottesville they should not have made Mr. Jefferson one of their number. Nonetheless, they acceded to his plan—after all, who could deny the ex-president when he spoke of establishing "the best seminary of the United States?"— and President Carr forwarded the letter, along with other related documents prepared by Jefferson, to David Watson of the Virginia legislature. As eventually presented, the petition to the General Assembly included, according to Patton: "the legal authority to demand and receive certain moneys which had arisen on the sale of the two glebes of the parishes of St. Ann and Fredericksville," (the two parishes which made up Albemarle County); a dividend "of the interest or profits of [the State Literary Fund] proportioned every year to the ratio which the contributors of the county bore to the rest of the State"; a reduction in the academy's number of trustees, called "visitors," and a definition of their "powers and duties"; and a change in the name of the educational institution, a change which would better reflect the proposed reorganization. The General Assembly gave their approval to the plan, minus the receipt of Literary Fund monies, in February of 1816. The second incarnation of the University of Virginia—Central College—was born.

"Be it enacted by the General Assembly that there be established in the county of Albemarle, at the place which has been, and shall be elected by the Trustees of Albemarle Academy, and in lieu of such academy, an institution for the education of youth, to be called The Central College. . . ." The institution would be funded by a liberal private subscription of up to $44,000, and was endowed by the state with the proceeds from the sale of certain glebe properties in Albemarle County's two parishes.

Jefferson's educational dreams for Virginia were beginning to gel. The University of Virginia's evolution into a state institution, wrote Adams, "is an unwritten chapter in American educational history. . . . There was absolutely nothing for Jefferson to build upon except an idea. It was impossible to make a State university out of old William and Mary College, which was then a church institution. There were not even common schools to render education popular. Jefferson had conceived the original idea of developing into a State university a county academy *which as yet existed only on paper* [emphasis in the original]. There was no endowment whatever. Everything had to be created."

The act creating Central College made Virginia's governor its patron, and gave him the power to appoint the Board of Visitors, numbering six, as well as fill its vacancies. The new appointees included Jefferson, then-president James Madison, future president James Monroe (his election would come later that year), David Watson, John Hartwell Cocke, and Joseph Carrington Cabell. These last two were especially instrumental in the college's metamorphosis into the University of Virginia. John Hartwell Cocke was the owner of Bremo, a large estate on the James River near present-day Scottsville. Well-known throughout central Virginia, Cocke had served as a general during the War of 1812 and published articles on agriculture and temperance. Also something of a maverick to his generation of Virginia slave-owners, Cocke advocated freeing slaves and paying them wages to work the fields. To Jefferson's plans for education he gave liberally of his money and talents. Cocke later helped supervise the construction of the University's original structures.

In the birthing of the University of Virginia, Joseph Carrington Cabell's importance was second only to Jefferson's. If the Sage of Monticello was U.Va.'s father, Cabell was certainly its midwife. Born in 1778, Joseph Carrington Cabell, like Jefferson, was a graduate of William and Mary and a lawyer. Like Jefferson, too, Cabell traveled through Europe and was greatly influenced by European culture and educational methods. Returning to the United States in 1807, he contacted President Jefferson regarding the idea of establishing a museum of natural history in Williamsburg, at their alma mater. "If the amelioration of education and the diffusion of knowledge be the favorite objects of your life," answered Jefferson through his private secretary, "avail yourself of the favorable dispositions of your countrymen, and consent to go into our legislative body. Instead of wasting your time in attempting to patch up a decaying institution, direct your efforts to a higher and more valuable object. Found a new one which shall be worthy of the first State of the Union. This may, this certainly will one day be done, and why not now? You may not succeed in one session, or in two, but you will succeed at last." Following Jefferson's advice, Cabell entered Virginia politics. "He became a member of the House of Delegates in 1809," wrote Adams, "and two years later was elected to the State Senate, where he remained until the year 1829, the most efficient champion of Jefferson's three great ideas—local government, popular education, and a State university. . . . [W]ithout Joseph Carrington Cabell's persistent labors in the Legislature, his self-sacrifice and indomitable courage, his wonderful political tact and unfailing diplomacy, Jefferson's university ideal would never have been realized, at least [not] in his lifetime."

Central College's Visitors met for the first time on April 8, 1817. Potential sites for the institution were visited and the one offered by John Perry was selected (and eventually purchased). Located a mile west of Charlottesville, the 200-acre site—which features a prominent ridge running north and south—was described by Jefferson as being "high, dry, open, furnished with good water, and [had] nothing in its vicinity which could threaten the health of the students." (This last attribute was a direct slap at William and Mary's location which many believed detrimental to the constitutions of its young scholars.)

With a well-selected Board of Visitors in place—and a promising location in hand—Jefferson went to work on Central College with a level of energy that belied his seventy-plus years. He performed all the tasks of a chief executive officer, and then some. He surveyed and laid out the site himself in July of 1817—using a theodolite, locust stakes, and twine—and planned and designed the buildings and grounds. At the May meeting, Mr. Jefferson presented the Visitors with a construction plan which featured, among other details, "a distinct pavilion or building for each separate professorship; these to be arranged around a square; each pavilion to contain a school-room and two apartments for the accommodation of the professor's family, and other reasonable conveniences. . . ." The pavilions, as later reported to the House of Delegates, would be connected "by a range of dormitories, capable each of lodging two students only— a provision equally friendly to study as to morals and order. . . . The plan . . . gave to the whole, in form and effect, the character of an academical village." The Board of Visitors selected a special construction committee—composed of Jefferson and Cocke—and instructed it to erect one of the pavilions at once.

The cornerstone of the first building, Pavilion VII, was laid during a solemn ceremony by the Charlottesville Lodge of Masons on October 6, 1817. According to the Richmond *Enquirer*, "a large company of citizens attended," including local shop owners, and the judges and attendees of the county and superior courts, then in session, who rushed to the ridge west of town. "They were animated," wrote U.Va. historian Philip Alexander Bruce, "some by an interest in learning, some by a spirit of diversion, and some, perhaps, by a desire to gaze at a group of three men composed of two former Presidents of the United States, Jefferson and Madison, and the present incumbent of that office, Monroe."

During this period, Cabell and other Jefferson supporters in the General Assembly were eagerly pushing for the establishment of a state university. Opposed to this plan were the alumni of William and Mary who believed their alma mater already held, and therefore could rightfully claim, the position of "The University of Virginia." But William and Mary—chartered in 1693—had fallen into disrepair since its days of prominence before the Revolution. Attendance was down and many people, including Jefferson as noted above, questioned whether its location—close to swampy land and its so-called miasmic vapors—was injurious to the health of its students.

A bill to set up a state university was approved by the General Assembly on February 21, 1818. The clause referring to the institution's location, however, was vague, simply saying that it should be "convenient and proper." In order to determine the site, therefore, a twenty-four-member commission—to meet at a tavern at Rockfish Gap in the Blue Ridge Mountains—was appointed by Gov. James Patton Preston. Cabell had used his influence to make sure that the commissioners would be chosen by the governor, rather than by the directors of the state Literary Fund, because he considered it an important first step in the designation of Charlottesville and he felt that Preston was more likely to select men who shared Jefferson's opinions.

The Rockfish Gap Commission—which included both Jefferson and James Madison as members—assembled for the first time on Saturday, August 1, 1818. It was tasked by the legislature with determining: the site for the University of Virginia; a plan for its construction; the branches of learning to be taught therein; the number of professorships; and the general, legislative provisions the institution would require for its organization and future government. "All these requirements," wrote Bruce, "were precisely in harmony with Jefferson's wishes, and they had quite probably been indirectly, through Cabell, proposed by him."

Interestingly, the conference's location, atop the Blue Ridge with its stunning views of both the Piedmont and the Shenandoah Valley, marked the perfect dividing line between the contending factions. And, despite the high-brow nature of the argument at hand, the commission's first session—in the tavern's crude dining hall, with only a rough table and well-used split-bottom chairs as furniture—most resembled a frontier assembly. Besides Charlottesville, the contenders were Staunton, and Lexington's Washington College which boasted a physical plant worth $25,000 and a wealthy Rockbridge County benefactor willing to cough up an additional $100,000. Naturally Jefferson, unanimously chosen to preside over the conference, backed the location nearest his home, and nearest his heart. Of the three sites, Jefferson explained, Charlottesville was closer to the Old Dominion's geographical center. It also more closely approximated the center of Virginia's white population. These points he ingeniously demonstrated with a large cardboard map of the Old Dominion—one which had constituted, according to Bruce, "the most esteemed part of his baggage in his journey to Rockfish Gap." Additionally, as pointed out by Jefferson, several buildings at Central College were already under construction, and Albemarle's climate was beneficial to the health of its residents. This last assertion he backed up by producing a long list of the county's resident octogenarians. After many hours of debate, the commission decided in favor of Charlottesville. When the findings were presented to the General Assembly, the arguments that had commenced at Rockfish Gap erupted anew. In the end, however, Joseph Cabell and Jefferson's other supporters—and Central College—won out. The Assembly granted the charter for the University of Virginia on January 25, 1819. "We have got possession of the ground," Cabell wrote Jefferson on February 4, "and it will never be taken from us."

The Visitors of Central College met for the last time on February 26. They decided that all available funds would go toward additional buildings. "We must apply all our funds to building for the present," wrote Jefferson, "and not open the institution until we can do it with that degree of splendor necessary to give it a prominent character." This last point was an important one for Jefferson. "The great object of our aim from the beginning," he later wrote to Cabell, "has been to make the [University] the most eminent in the United States. . . . We have proposed, therefore, to call to it characters of the first order of science from Europe, as well as our own country, and not only by the salaries . . . but by the distinguished scale of its structure and preparation. . . . Had we built a barn for a college and log huts for accommodations, should we ever had the assurance to propose to a European professor of that character to come to it?" The Visitors agreed—this architectural point-of-view was essential because tiny Charlottesville, and its environs, had little to recommend it to either prospective faculty or students.

The Board of Visitors of the University of Virginia met for the first time on March 29, 1819. Present were Thomas Jefferson, James Madison, Joseph Carrington Cabell, John Hartwell Cocke, Chapman Johnson, James Breckenridge and Robert B. Taylor. The first four of these gentlemen had been Visitors of Central College. They appointed a bursar, set compensation for professors, and agreed that all available monies should go toward the ongoing construction. They also elected Jefferson the University's first rector. "Henceforth, until his death in 1826," wrote Adams, "Jefferson was the directing and shaping power in the upbuilding of the University of Virginia. Never was an institution more completely the materialization of one man's thought. . . ." On the cleared ridge west of Charlottesville, those ideas were finally taking form.

The physical construction of the University, as noted above, had begun in 1817, even though the buildings were intended for an institution then-named Central College. In planning the layout, Jefferson—a self-taught architect—requested suggestions and illustrations from both Dr. William Thornton, a gentleman amateur like himself, and Benjamin H. Latrobe, an English-born architect who was working at the time on the restoration of the U.S. Capitol. Jefferson incorporated one of Thornton's sketches into his design for Pavilion VII. Two of Latrobe's suggestions for the general site plan, however, proved far more useful. An 1817 Latrobe sketch shows both pavilions "exhibiting," he wrote, "different types or orders of architecture," plus a round central building "which ought to exhibit in mass and details as perfect a specimen of good architectural taste as can be desired." The drawing, in fact, includes a thumbnail sketch of a rotunda that closely resembles Jefferson's final design. Jefferson adopted Latrobe's suggestions—incorporating, as they did, classical architecture—because they fit his concept of basing the University on the ancient Greek practices of education. In Jefferson's original plan the professors lived upstairs in the pavilions and taught their classes on the ground floors. Their charges, of course, lived alongside in the Lawn rooms. In homage to the Greeks, therefore, teachers and students were gathered physically as well as intellectually. At the time this concept was considered thoroughly unique—few contemporaries thought it could succeed.

For the University's classical design Jefferson revisited the work of the sixteenth-century Italian architect who had initially inspired the creation of Monticello—Andrea Palladio. Reprinted in 1742, Palladio's *The Four Books of Architecture* contain a complete description of the classical orders plus detailed illustrations revealing how best to adapt them to public and private buildings. In developing his plans for the University's structures, Jefferson pored over Palladio's drawings, carefully reproducing the proper forms and proportions.

Jefferson, it will be remembered, had surveyed the site atop the prominent north-to-south ridge on July 18, 1817. He was then seventy-four years old. In his pocket notebook the elder statesman that day sketched a diagram of the future grounds. Around a central open space—which he staked out as three terraces he called "squares"—Jefferson located the sites for six large, two-story pavilions. The first pavilion to be built, number VII, he placed in the center of the western edge's middle square. On the northern extent of the grounds he marked the spot where he desired "some principal building" be erected. The ridge was leveled in the latter part of July, and the cornerstone of Pavilion VII was laid on October 6.

The original idea of erecting six, two-story pavilions Jefferson soon expanded to encompass ten. The plan as finally adopted runs along three sides of an elongated, rectangular green—Jefferson's Lawn—which covers nearly two acres. The rectangle's long sides feature parallel rows of five pavilions each—the East and West Lawns—connected by one-story Tuscan colonnades. Behind these reside the single-chamber student rooms, fifty-four in all—twenty-eight along the West Lawn and twenty-six on the East Lawn. Calling these dormitories "monkish cells," historian Herbert B. Adams wrote that the colonnades "remind one of cloistered walks in some ancient monastery." Interspersed between the student "cells," the ten, red brick pavilions—all in the Federal style—look down on the Lawn through wonderful classical facades. Jefferson choose a separate classical order for each so that they could serve as architectural models. He exhibited the various orders in the following manner:

> Pavilion I, the Doric Order of Diocletian's Baths, Chambray,
> Pavilion II, the Ionic Order of Fortuna Virilis,
> Pavilion III, the Corinthian Order of Palladio,
> Pavilion IV, the Doric Order of Albano,
> Pavilion V, Palladio's Ionic Order with modillions,
> Pavilion VI, the Ionic Order of the Theatre of Marcellus,
> Pavilion VII, the Doric Order of Palladio,
> Pavilion VIII, the Corinthian Order of Diocletian's Baths,
> Pavilion IX, the Ionic Order of the Temple of Fortuna Virilis, and
> Pavilion X, the Doric Order of the Theatre of Marcellus.

The Lawn's southern side was originally left open while its northern boundary—its highest point—was the last to see construction.

The construction advanced fairly quickly under Jefferson and Cocke's supervision. By mid December of 1819, the brickwork of the five West Lawn pavilions, along with that of their adjacent student rooms, had been completed. Opposite them on the East Lawn, two pavilions were standing. The building report of 1821 listed the following structures as being "in readiness for occupation" except for a bit of plastering: "ten distinct houses or pavilions containing each a lecturing room . . . ; six hotels for dieting the students . . . ; and a hundred and nine dormitories, sufficient each for the accommodation of two students, arranged in four distinct rows between the pavilions and hotels. . . ." The two outer rows of student rooms—the East and West Ranges—were erected 100 yards on either side, and parallel to, the East and West Lawn. Unlike the Lawn rooms, these dormitories were set behind brick arcades. Each of the ranges also included three two-story brick buildings—Hotels A through F—which served as dining halls.

Most of the bricks for the University's original structures were made on the grounds, at a large brickyard facing the West Range. The red, central Virginia clay was first dug, then piled into large heaps for winter weathering. In the spring the clay was mixed with sand, hand-molded, and kiln-dried. Jefferson sometimes oversaw work at the brickyard, which, at its peak, turned out 180,000 bricks per month.

The initial funds for the University of Virginia came from the state Literary Fund. Established in 1810, the Fund had set aside $15,000 to benefit the state university. Another $40,000 was available that had been collected for Central College, while the sale of glebe lands had netted only 3,000 more. These monies were sufficient to continue construction—once the charter had been granted—but were hardly enough to complete the University. Undaunted, Jefferson redoubled his efforts to raise funds. Cabell, however, at a low point in the struggle decided to retire from the Legislature, writing Jefferson in 1821 that his object henceforth would be "domestic, rural, and literary leisure." The seventy-eight-year-old "Sage of Monticello" was unyielding in his reply. "The gloomiest of all prospects," he wrote, "is in the desertion of the best friends of the institution; for desertion I must call it.... What object of our lives can we propose so important? What interest of our own which ought not to be postponed to this? If any member of our college of Visitors could justifiably withdraw from this sacred duty, it would be myself, who . . . have neither vigor of body or mind left to keep the field. But I will die in the last ditch. And so I hope you will, my friend. . . ." Cabell confessed that "It is not in my nature to resist such an appeal." In the end, a loan of $180,000 from the state Literary Fund was necessary to complete the buildings of the Lawn and the East and West Ranges. Eventually, the General Assembly forgave the debt, and appropriated an additional $50,000 to erect the capstone of Jefferson's "academical village"—the Rotunda.

Construction of the "sphere within a cylinder"—as Jefferson referred to his "principal building" at the rectangle's northern edge—was begun in October of 1822. Using one of Palladio's sketchbooks, Jefferson based his Rotunda on the Roman Pantheon, a temple to all the gods. Not wanting it to dwarf the nearest pavilions, however, he scaled down the size and reduced the number of columns from eight to six. The upper level, the dome room, was created to hold the school's first library. When the University opened it featured something over 6,000 titles from a list Jefferson had written out by hand. The two lower levels were designed as classrooms and meeting halls.

Jefferson devoted all the energies of his final years to the University of Virginia. Tradition holds, for example, that in 1819 the ex-president, then seventy-six, designed all of the five East Lawn Pavilions in approximately fifteen days—an amazing average of only three days per structure. He would also frequently ride down from Monticello to oversee the workmen's efforts. "Our University, four miles distant," he wrote John Adams in 1820, "gives me frequent exercise, and the oftener, as I direct its architecture." When he could not personally supervise the work he would train his looking glass—mounted on Monticello's north terrace walk—on the construction site. He was particularly interested in his beautiful domed Rotunda. It was in the Rotunda's dome room—still unfinished—that the Marquis de Lafayette was feted at an elaborate dinner on November 5, 1824. Filled to overflowing with 400 guests, the dome that day resounded with numerous tributes to Jefferson and the French-born hero of the Revolution. The Rotunda was completed in September of 1826, making it the last of Jefferson's buildings erected. Unfortunately, the author of the Declaration had died two months earlier on July 4—the fiftieth anniversary of that document's adoption—and never saw his Rotunda as a finished work.

When the University of Virginia finally opened its doors in March of 1825, eight of the desired professorships had been filled. Much like the structures of Mr. Jefferson's Lawn, these intellectuals were a decidedly unique collection—six of them were not Americans. When early efforts to engage prominent U.S. educators failed, Francis Gilmer—a well-educated Albemarle native—had been dispatched to England and Scotland to bring back a teaching staff. From Cambridge University came Englishmen George Long and Thomas H. Key. Long occupied the chair of ancient languages, while Key held that of mathematics. Robley Dunglison, also English-born, had been contracted to teach medicine. It was Dunglison who attended Jefferson at his death bed and later became known as the 'father of physiology." Charles Bonnycastle had traveled the Atlantic to occupy the chair of natural philosophy—or physics—while Irishman John Emmett had come up from Charleston, S.C., to give courses on the same subject. George Blaetterman, a German, was hired to lecture on modern languages. Virginian John Tayloe Lomax was the University's first professor of law and George Tucker—another Virginian and a member of Congress—held the chair of moral philosophy. Tucker became the first chairman of the faculty.

The entering class in 1825 was but forty students, a number that would rise to 116 within a year. When these young University of Virginia scholars first strode the Lawn they quickly realized that Mr. Jefferson had not just founded an educational institution, he had also created an incredibly beautiful architectural legacy. This he had accomplished despite the seemingly insurmountable difficulties of old age, monetary uncertainty, and political squabbling. It was the noblest work of Jefferson's life. "I have long been sensible," he once wrote to Cabell, "that while I was endeavoring to render our country the greatest of all services . . . I was discharging the odious function of a physician pouring medicine down the throat of the patient insensible of needing it. I am so sure of the future approbation of posterity, and of the inestimable effect we shall have produced in the elevation of our country by what we have done, as that I can not repent of the part I have borne in co-operation with my colleagues."

The ruins of Barboursville, in Orange County.
(Photo by the author.)

XII

"A Sage and a Man of Taste":
Jefferson's Architectural Legacy

"As for the beauty of an edifice, it consists of an exact proportion of the parts within themselves, and of each part with the whole: for a fine building ought to appear as an entire and perfect body, wherein every member agrees with its fellow, and each so well with the whole, that it may seem absolutely necessary to the being of the same."
- Italian Architect Andrea Palladio (1508–80)

After an extensive breakfast of fresh eggs, ham, milk, and coffee the entourage departed Boswell's Tavern and rode west. Heading the party was forty-eight-year-old François-Jean, Marquis de Chastellux, a professional soldier holding the rank of major general in General Jean Baptiste Rochambeau's army—the French expeditionary force that had participated in the siege of Yorktown. More importantly, perhaps, Chastellux was also a man of letters and a distinguished member of the French Academy.

The company proceeded slowly—Chastellux and the three other officers at the front followed by their seven body servants riding horses piled high with baggage. After a short distance they encountered an Irish horse-trader from North Carolina who graciously consented to guide them further into Albemarle County. The region was sparsely populated and the dense woods on either side of the track disguised their approach to the Southwest Mountains. And so they talked. Chastellux was particularly interested in the Irishman's description of his adopted home and his methods of doing business. It was the early afternoon of April 13, 1782.

Suddenly they found themselves at the base of a mountain range. "We had no difficulty in recognizing on one of the summits the house of Mr. Jefferson," Chastellux remembered in his *Travels in North America* published four years later, "for it may be said that 'it shines alone in this secluded spot.'" When the Frenchmen ascended the "little mountain," Chastellux was tremendously impressed by Thomas Jefferson's home, and the marvelous view of the country all around. "He himself built it and chose the site," he wrote. "But Nature so contrived it, that a Sage and a man of taste should find on his own estate the spot where he might best study and enjoy Her." (Jefferson could not have agreed more. "How sublime to look down into the workhouse of nature," he wrote, "to see her clouds, hail, snow, rain, thunder, all fabricated at our feet!")

"[Jefferson] called this house Monticello," continued Chastellux, "a name which bespeaks the owner's attachment to the language of Italy and above all to the Fine Arts. . . . [His house] resembles none of the others seen in this country; so that it may be said that Mr. Jefferson is the first American who has consulted the Fine Arts to know how he should shelter himself from the weather."

"A man of many interests, not the least of them architecture," wrote architectural historian K. Edward Lay, "Jefferson designed in his native county two of the world's great examples of the building arts: a dwelling, Monticello, and an institution of higher learning, the University of Virginia." But he also designed—or assisted in the design of—a number of other structures in Virginia. His architectural influence on his native state—and indeed on the nation—was immense. "One can argue," noted Lay, "that no other American architect has surpassed Jefferson in his influence on the built environment of the United States. Just as every writer of fiction . . . has since the time of Shakespeare written either in emulation of or in reaction to the bard, so has it been with the Classical Revival idiom that Jefferson introduced to his fellow countrymen. . . ." This Jefferson accomplished despite his over thirty-five years in public service, and his pursuit of a great number of other fascinations. Some of his architectural gems, unfortunately, are now gone—they were either torn down or consumed by fire—but many still remain, scattered all across the Old Dominion. They seem, as historian Desmond Guinness has so aptly worded, "peculiarly at home in the brilliant Virginia sun."

"Few activities interested [Jefferson] more than building," wrote Jefferson biographer Dumas Malone, "and it is unfortunate that the scanty early records do not reveal just when this interest was manifested first." Perhaps as a young boy he was attracted to the study of architecture while observing construction undertaken at Shadwell by his father, Peter Jefferson. Perhaps his first great influence was Richard Taliaferro—at the time considered Virginia's leading architect—a man young Jefferson became acquainted with in Williamsburg. (Taliaferro was the father-in-law of George Wythe, under whom Jefferson read the law.) From an early age Jefferson displayed a need to control—a need to both systematize and categorize his surroundings. This inner drive to organize the physical world—as also witnessed by his great love of science—impelled him quite naturally toward architecture. "Jefferson's awareness of the uncertainty of life and the swift passage of time," wrote Lay, "compelled him to organize himself, impose order on his day, and control his environment. All of these needs and impulses found their outlet in the practice of architecture."

Jefferson's lifelong pursuit of architecture was very much in keeping with the Renaissance tradition, as it was being practiced in England at the time by "gentlemen amateurs." As architecture did not yet exist in the Americas as a profession, young Jefferson—as a beginning amateur—looked to Europe for inspiration. Eighteenth-century European architects, in turn, were looking to the ancient world for their inspiration and thus created the Classical Revival period of architecture. Many of these men published pattern books or reissued older architectural works that tremendously influenced their American counterparts. Some of the most important such works included *The Architecture of A. Palladio; in Four Books*—re-released by Giacomo Leoni between 1716 and 1720—James Gibbs's *Book of Architecture* (1728), William Salmon's *Palladio Londinensis* (1734), and Robert Morris's *Select Architecture* (1755).

Sixteenth-century Italian architect Andrea Palladio (c.1510–c.1589) became Jefferson's first great architectural mentor. Jefferson was quoted as referring to Palladio's *Four Books*, in fact, as "the Bible." Palladio had closely examined, measured, and illustrated the stately buildings of the Roman Empire, in the process becoming the absolute master of the noblest ideas of the ancients. His subsequent designs stressed harmonic proportions and classical symmetry. But whereas Palladio held first rank in Jefferson's architectural thinking, "Robert Morris, who designed buildings in spheres and perfect cubes," penned historian Noble E. Cunningham, Jr., "also appealed to Jefferson's mathematical mind. He liked the simplicity of Morris's designs and their adaptability to small scale." Although Jefferson's knowledge of architecture came primarily from pattern books—and his later experiences in Europe as a "savage from the wilds of Virginia"—the master of Monticello developed into much more than a mere copyist.

Another great influence on his architectural point-of-view was the dearth of what Jefferson considered worthy—or even acceptable—architecture in the Old Dominion. Some of his earliest statements on the topic are found in his *Notes On the State of Virginia*, written in the early 1780s. It was there that he registered his disgust in Virginia's architectural state of affairs. "The only public buildings [in Virginia] worthy of mention," he wrote, "are the Capitol, the Palace, the College [of William and Mary], and the Hospital for Lunatics, all of them in Williamsburg, heretofore the seat of our government. The Capitol is a light and airy structure . . . [but] [t]he College and Hospital are rude, mis-shapen piles, which, but that they have roofs, would be taken for brick-kilns. There are no other public buildings but churches and courthouses in which attempts are made at elegance. . . ."

"The genius of architecture seems to have shed its maledictions over this land," continued Jefferson. "Buildings are often erected, by individuals, of considerable expence [*sic*]. To give these symmetry and taste would not increase their cost. . . . But the first principles of

the art are unknown. . . . Architecture being one of the fine arts . . .
perhaps a spark may fall on some young subjects of natural taste,
kindle up their genius, and produce a reformation in this elegant
and useful art."

Perhaps not surprisingly, the "reformation" of architecture
in Virginia was soon thereafter led by Jefferson himself—for the
"spark" had fallen on him while serving as American minister to
France (1785–89). There he was greatly influenced by the new
architecture, "returning home," according to Cunningham, "with
his Palladian views much altered by the Louis XVI style. He
was especially enthralled by Paris's beautiful *hotels* (mansions or
townhouses) designed by leading architects during a period of great
architectural creativity." "Were I to proceed to tell you how much
I enjoy French architecture," Jefferson wrote Charles Bellini in
1785, "I should want words." Two years later, in a letter to Madame
Tesse, the Marquis de Lafayette's aunt, Jefferson described his
overwhelming appreciation for two French structures. "Here I am,
Madame, gazing whole hours at the *Maison Quarree*, like a lover
at his mistress. . . . While at Paris, I was violently smitten with the
Hotel de Salm, and used to go to the *Tuileries* almost daily to look at
it. The *loueuse des chaises* [woman renting chairs], inattentive to my
passion, never had the complaisance to place a chair there, so that,
sitting on the parapet, and twisting my neck round to see the object
of my admiration, I generally left with a torticollis [or stiff neck].
From Lyons to Nimes I have been nourished with the remains of
Roman Grandeur."

Back in Virginia, following his sojourn in France, Jefferson put
to good use his fascination with what he called "this elegant and
useful art." Jefferson's "consuming interest in architecture began,
not with his concern for culture," according to Malone, "but with
his desire to engage in actual construction, or to help his friends do
so." In the years after his return in 1789—notwithstanding the years
spent serving the nation and creating the University of Virginia—
Jefferson found the time to design three homes for his family and

friends: Edgemont, near Alberene in southern Albemarle County; Edgehill near Shadwell, where Jefferson was born; and Barboursville in Orange County to the northeast.

Edgemont—attributed to Jefferson because of its similarity to other homes he designed—was constructed for Col. James Powell Cocke in 1796. Born in 1748 in Henrico County, where he served as a justice, Cocke had moved to Albemarle in search of a healthier clime. "Edgement, based on Andrea Palladio's Villa Capra (Rotunda) in Vicenza," wrote Lay, "is a bank house: one story at its entrance, which is centered on a hill to the south, but dropping off to two stories to the north, which faces its parterres [or ornamental gardens]." Because the home sits on the edge of a slope, visitors approaching the west front portico, or carriage entrance, see but one level. From the east front, or garden entrance, both stories are visible. All told, however, Edgemont has four porticoes. Those on the north and south lead out onto elevated terraces which terminate in flanking pavilions.

Jefferson preferred solid buildings of brick and stone, writing that "[a] country whose buildings are of wood, can never increase in its improvements to any considerable degree." Despite this preference, however, Edgemont was constructed in wood. "Edgement's rusticated frame walls were originally 'sanded' [or coated with sand]," penned Lay, "and the joints painted in a contrasting color to make the walls look like stone." Guinness described Edgemont as having "the elegance of a palace and the simplicity of a cottage . . . a perfect example of how purity of line can be used to best advantage." That "purity of line" represented Jefferson's simple understatement of the Palladian villa. The house passed through many hands following the death of Colonel Cocke until, fortuitously, it was beautifully restored in the mid-1900s.

First proposed by Jefferson in 1790—at the marriage of his oldest daughter Martha to Thomas Mann Randolph, Jr.—Edgehill was actually begun eight years later. The plan for the "small, wooden, one-story Tuscan villa," wrote Bryan Clark Green, "was drawn by Jefferson and was his preference for the house. Its awkward room arrangement, however, led Jefferson in the end to adopt instead" a T-shaped plan. Randolph, thanks to his many years in public service—two terms in the U.S. Congress and three as Virginia governor—was often absent from Edgehill. Following his death in 1828, his son Thomas Jefferson Randolph—Jefferson's favorite grandson—finding Edgehill too small for his purposes replaced it with a larger, two-story brick structure that still survives. According to one source, the second version of Edgehill—designed by Thomas R. Blackburn—was built directly atop the foundations of the original.

Jefferson designed Barboursville for Gov. James Barbour circa 1817. Barbour—who had also served as U.S. senator, secretary of war, and minister to England—had written Jefferson in March of that year: "I have resolved on the plan you were good enough to present me and for which I return my sincere thanks. You . . . [suggested] that it would be well for my workmen to see your building and receive such verbal explanations as might facilitate their labors." To that end brick mason Edward Ancel and carpenter James Bradley soon thereafter visited Jefferson's home, and probably also the early structures at the University of Virginia.

Understandably, many of Barboursville's features were reminiscent of those employed by Jefferson at Monticello. A two-story building, it appeared to the casual observer to be a single-story home. Rising up the the portico was a turf ramp—reminiscent of Monticello's garden entrance—which added to the illusion. Like Jefferson's home, the upstairs windows were placed close to those immediately below so as to disguise the second story. And the initial plan included a dome—which was, however, never constructed. Like Monticello too, both the entrance hall and drawing rooms were two stories high—flanked by square rooms separated by narrow hallways—and the octagonal drawing room projected out onto the garden portico. Exhibiting his well-known disdain for grand central staircases, Jefferson gave Barboursville two flights of steps located in the transverse passages. Unfortunately the home burned on Christmas Day, 1884. All that remains are a few brick walls and the sentinel-like two-story columns.

Jefferson's architectural savvy influenced the design of several other Virginia mansions. These include Montpelier in Orange County, the home of James and Dolley Madison; Farmington west of Charlottesville, owned by George Divers; James Monroe's Oak Hill, in Leesburg, Loudoun County; and Upper Bremo on the James River in Fluvanna County, the home of Gen. John Hartwell Cocke.

The original section of Montpelier was constructed in the mid-eighteenth century by James Madison Sr., the president's father. In 1793, James Madison the younger requested building advice from Jefferson just prior to marrying Dolley and enlarging his home. The two had already corresponded on the subject of architecture. "But how is a taste in this beautiful art to be formed in our countrymen," Jefferson had written Madison in 1785, "unless we avail ourselves of every occasion when public buildings are to be erected, of presenting to them models for their study and imitation? You see I am an enthusiast on the subject of the arts. But it is an enthusiasm of which I am not ashamed, as its object is to improve the taste of my countrymen, to increase their reputation, to reconcile them to the rest of the world, and procure them its praise." Evidence seems to indicate that Jefferson designed Montpelier's great portico—which architectural historian Fiske Kimball called "Jeffersonian in suggestion as well as in proportions"—and Madison's Tuscan temple icehouse. (Jefferson may have also provided plans and "general notes" which led to the ultimate creation of Woodberry Forest, owned by Madison's brother.)

Farmington sits atop a broad knoll approximately five miles west of Monticello. Jefferson's neighbor, and fellow horticulturist, George Divers—Dr. Thomas Walker's son-in-law—purchased the estate, which came with a modest two-story house, in 1785. Seventeen years later, in 1802, he determined to enlarge the home and wrote to President Jefferson for advice. Jefferson's plan for Farmington included a large, attached wing in the shape of an elongated octagon—the president at the time was experimenting with octagons—which would be entered through a Doric-styled portico.

Overwhelmed with the duties of the presidency, Jefferson of course was not able to oversee construction at Farmington. "The result," wrote Lay, "was not to his satisfaction: columns were out of proportion, and the demi-octagonal ends lacked a full entablature around them. The interior was built as a asymmetrical space with an off set partition." Unfortunately, Divers died during the reconstruction of Farmington and the Jeffersonian addition was not completed until fifty years later. Subsequent owners made significant changes.

Oak Hill in Northern Virginia was built for then-president James Monroe in 1819. Monroe evidently sought Jefferson's advice during construction, for the "Sage of Monticello" wrote, in June of 1820: "Instead of the unintelligible sketch I gave you the other day, I send it drawn more at large. Mrs. Monroe and yourself may take some hints from it for a better plan of your own. . . ." The home originally featured a massive five-column portico overlooking formal terraced gardens. In the 1920s large wings were added to either side of the building, greatly reducing the visual effect once produced by the tall pillars.

Upper Bremo—more commonly called simply Bremo—was built between 1817 and 1820 for John Hartwell Cocke, a close friend of Jefferson's. Cocke had served as a brigadier general in the War of 1812, and was senior vice president of the American Colonization Society, president of the National Temperance Union, and commissioner of roads for Virginia. He later served on the University of Virginia's Board of Visitors for thirty-three years.

Bremo's design was at first attributed to Jefferson. A later study, however, proved it to be the creation of John Neilson, a "superior house-joiner" who, along with James Dinsmore, had worked closely with Jefferson on his seemingly endless reconstruction of Monticello. Nonetheless, Jefferson's influences can be seen throughout. They include, according to Lay: "twenty-foot cubic spaces, dependencies recessed into the hillside, upper windows at floor level to reduce the apparent scale, bed alcoves, a rotating food-serving door, and small stairs tucked away." Also like Monticello, the central building is connected to twin pavilions—created as exterior offices—by long, wooden-railed terraces. The entrance portico resembles that of Jefferson's home, although its columns are of the simpler Tuscan order—rather than the Doric—wrote Guinness, "in deference to General Cocke's austere taste."

Bremo's grounds feature pisé, or rammed-earth buildings— probably Virginia's first—diamond-notched log structures, and several stone outbuildings. Of special interest is Bremo's circa 1816 classical stone barn—perhaps the nation's only such example. Fiske Kimball called Bremo "artistic perfection." Unlike Monticello, which was drastically remodeled, "Bremo has the inevitability of a single ordered creation," he wrote. "Calm, monumental and serene, it commands our emotion as a masterpiece of the art form."

Among other Virginia homes influenced by Jefferson are Moldavia in Richmond—at Sixth and Cary streets—and Mount Athos in Campbell County. Begun in 1798, Moldavia—which, according to Green, "unites the names of its first owners, Molly and David Meade Randolph—was designed by George Winston, a well-known Richmond contractor, and constructed in brick. It originally sat on an entire Richmond city block. The Randolphs' fortunes, however, were fleeting. "The rich miller Joseph Gallego and his wife bought Moldavia in 1804," wrote Green, "and in 1805 hired James Oldham, one of Thomas Jefferson's workmen, to enlarge the building. Then-president Jefferson, after lending Oldham a copy of Palladio's *Four Books of Architecture*, advised on the project himself."

Moldavia's original section—the southern side—featured a two-tiered piazza and a semi-octagonal bow with a marvelous view of the mighty James. "It appears that Gallego added the northerly wing of the house to hold his drawing room," continued Green. "In the contest of styles, this room represented an opportunity to Jefferson, who treated new buildings as chances to reform architecture by setting models, particularly models of the orders." In 1805 President Jefferson wrote Oldham of the order he intended for the drawing room—the Corinthian—explaining that "a single example of chaste architecture may guide the taste of a city." In 1825 Moldavia was purchased by wealthy merchant John Allan, whose foster son Edgar Allan Poe lived there briefly before attending Jefferson's University of Virginia in 1826. Sadly, this Jefferson-influenced home was demolished circa 1890.

Built around 1800 for William J. Lewis, Mount Athos—with its classical portico, apparent one-story design, semi-octagonal projections, and scenic location above the James River—has been considered by many to be another brainchild of Jefferson's. According to Lewis family lore, William Lewis was a friend of Jefferson's and the "Sage of Monticello" advised him on his home's construction. It was built in stone rather than brick. Mount Athos burned in 1876 but its ruins remain.

By the time Moldavia and Mount Athos were being constructed, of course, Jefferson had already spent much time and expense in the construction of his own habitations. Monticello—discussed at length in another chapter—because of his once-stated enjoyment in "putting up and pulling down," was forty years in the making. "My essay in Architecture has been so much subordinated to the law of convenience," he wrote Benjamin Latrobe, "that it is liable to some unfavorable and just criticisms." When completed in 1809, Jefferson had finally created a home, wrote Dumas Malone, "befitting his extraordinarily diverse and well-rounded personality."

Poplar Forest—in Bedford County, Virginia, ninety miles from Monticello—had been designed in 1806 during his second term as president. The home is an octagon with fifty-foot-long sides. (Two years earlier Jefferson had envisioned creating an octagonal home at Pantops for his younger daughter Maria, the wife of John W. Eppes. Unfortunately, Maria died that very year from the complications of childbirth and the home was never built.)

Jefferson based the design of Poplar Forest—America's first octagonal home—upon a plate in William Kent's 1727 *Designs of Inigo Jones*. The home's central, two-story space—the dining room—is surrounded by four elongated octagonal rooms. Two of these, created as bedrooms, were divided by sleeping alcoves that could be entered from either side, much like that in Jefferson's own bedroom at Monticello. "Poplar Forest features a rear façade that demonstrates the first use of a portico over an arcade," wrote Lay. Unfortunately, this unique structure was gutted by fire in 1845 and substantially altered when reconstructed. The home has been restored to its original design, however, and—like Monticello—is currently open for public viewing.

Fortunately for the state of Virginia, Thomas Jefferson did not reserve his architectural talent exclusively for the design of homes, but also applied it liberally toward the construction of public buildings. His most famous public work, of course, is the University of Virginia (described in another chapter). He fashioned the original buildings so they would serve as "models in architecture of the purest forms of antiquity, furnishing to the student examples of the precepts he will be taught in that art." His beautiful "academical village" has been fascinating visitors since it first opened in 1825.

Other public edifices created by Jefferson include the Virginia State Capitol and three county courthouses—all examples of the Classical Revival Style, first begun in Virginia in the 1780s. "Its high-style manifestation," wrote Lay, "was the more literal and obvious inclusion of Roman temple elements. . . . Spurning the

Georgian model (in part due to anti-British sentiment), its adherents reached further back in times for inspiration to the 'original' and 'pure' wellsprings of classical architecture—the Greek and Roman republics. . . . Thomas Jefferson was the first and principal advocate of the new style, which he introduced in his plan for the Virginia State Capitol in Richmond."

Jefferson first executed a design for the capitol building in 1784, just prior to leaving for service abroad. The massive structure, when completed, was similar in many aspects. When in France Jefferson commissioned architect C. L. A. Clérisseau to produce a model from his plans. This was shipped to Richmond in 1786 together with detailed plans for the interior. "The Capitol in the city of Richmond," wrote Jefferson, "is the model of the Temples of Erectheus at Athens or Balbec, and the *Maison Carrée* of Nimes. All of which are nearly of the same form and proportions and are considered as the most perfect examples of cubic architecture. . . ." Subsequent additions and alterations have cumulatively changed the capitol so that it no longer represents, in pure form, Jefferson's ideal of the "public" temple.

In 1821 Charles Yancey wrote Jefferson on behalf of the Buckingham County commissioners. "I have taken liberty to trespass upon your time and talents (a common stock) which we all have the right to draw upon," penned Yancey to the seventy-eight-year-old ex-president, "to draft for us a plan of our Court house." Jefferson, of course, complied—only two weeks later!—with a hand-drawn plan, including measurements, and an explanatory note. "Everything proposed in them is in the plainest style, and will be cheap," penned Jefferson, "altho' requiring skill in the workmanship. . . . I cannot but therefore recommend to you to get the work undertaken by some of the workmen of our University." Following Jefferson's recommendations, the courthouse was built in 1822 by former University of Virginia brick mason Dabney Cosby. The completed building measured fifty-nine by forty-four feet, and included a Tuscan portico, columns built of brick plastered over, and three jury rooms. The courthouse was in constant use until 1869, when it burned.

Jefferson designed the Botetourt County Courthouse in 1818. In that year he wrote Gen. James Breckenridge, who later supervised the courthouse's erection, "I have been able to compleat [*sic*], and now to forward [the drawings] by mail with the explanations accompanying them, I hope your workmen will sufficiently understand them." Unfortunately, in 1847 the Botetourt County Courthouse—like that in Buckingham—was destroyed by fire. The Charlotte County Courthouse, built in 1823, was probably also created by the ex-president because it was later described as "built on a plan furnished by Mr. Jefferson." These three courthouses are wonderful examples of Jefferson's use of ancient Greek and Roman styles—his Classical Revivalism—and his adaptation of them for American civic purposes. "These three buildings," noted Green, "were enormously important because of their influence on the rural landscape of central Virginia. Some fifteen other county courthouses repeat the type."

Homes, courthouses, a university, and a capitol—quite a list of wonderful creations, and all from the hand of a man already over tasked with the burdens of public office, and a overabundant wealth of other interests. They represent a cultural and architectural legacy of which the Old Dominion can be proud.

Monticello's gorgeous West Portico.
(Photo by the author.)

XIII

SECURING A SHRINE:

The Early Years of the
Thomas Jefferson Memorial Foundation

Mount Vernon is preserved, and will continue to be a perpetual
inspiration. . . . [John Marshall 's home] has just been saved by the city
of Richmond, and there remains upon the crest of the Virginia hills
that historic edifice in which lived the man who was not only the pen
of the Revolution, but . . . more profoundly affected its development . . .
than any political leader since his death.

        - The Honorable James M. Beck,
        Assist. U.S. Attorney General, July 18, 1912

Mrs. Martin W. Littleton, wife of a prominent New York Democratic representative, stood in the crowd at Arlington National Cemetery, anxious to see the monument about to be dedicated to Washington architect Pierre Charles L'Enfant. A sea of white headstones completely flooded the surrounding field. The year was 1911. As the speakers droned on—President William H. Taft, New York Senator Elihu Root, and the French Ambassador—Littleton's eyes wandered across the wide Potomac to the marble-faced obelisk honoring the "Father of our Country." George Washington had been memorialized, and now L'Enfant was receiving his due, thought Mrs. Littleton, but nowhere in "this glorious temple of trees and marble" was there reserved a spot for Thomas Jefferson. Something must be done!

In August of that year Mrs. Littleton published an emotionally charged open letter entitled *One Wish*, which she distributed to her husband's influential friends. "It was [Jefferson] who had faith in man," she wrote. "It was *he* who fought for a New Government. . . . It was *he* who built an asylum for the oppressed of all nations. It was *he* who caused the separation of Church and State. . . . It was *he* who spoke the first words in behalf of the freedom of the Negroes. . . ." Jefferson belonged not only to the American people, she continued, "but to the people of all the world wherever liberty is."

Her one wish? That, in order to properly honor Thomas Jefferson, "the nation, whom he loved so well, [would] purchase and preserve forever the house and grounds and graveyard at Monticello," so that Americans would be *free* to lay upon his grave a nation's tears." The response to Littleton's missive was electric . . . but a very large obstacle stood in the way. That impediment was Jefferson Monroe Levy, Monticello's owner—he wasn't interested in selling. The following year Mrs. Littleton founded the Monticello Memorial Association and lobbied Congress to acquire the property. The fight to secure Jefferson's home as a national shrine was on.

That struggle would consume many more years, and the fundraising efforts of dozens of individuals nationwide. Unfortunately Littleton's organization died in the process but its standard—its one wish—was picked up and carried to victory by the Thomas Jefferson Memorial Foundation, her philosophical inheritor. The organization overcame seemingly insurmountable obstacles during its early years, and in the process reintroduced to America the Virginian whose life and principles guided our revolution and shaped our republic.

In the first two decades of the twentieth century several unsuccessful attempts had been made to purchase Monticello from Levy. In the early months of 1923, however, the time finally seemed right. The Thomas Jefferson Memorial Foundation—TJMF—was incorporated in Albany, New York on April 13, 1923, the "Sage of Monticello's" one hundred and eightieth birthday. The non-profit organization was set up, according to its 1926 report, "for the purpose of establishing Monticello as a memorial to the Author of the Declaration and . . . inculcating through patriotic education a better understanding and appreciation of the life and service of Thomas Jefferson." Formal announcement of the organization's existence appeared in the April 5 edition of *The New York Times*. In Charlottesville the Foundation's plans were first elaborated to a crowd of 500 assembled for Founder's Day exercises in Cabell Hall at the University of Virginia.

The Foundation's original composition was an eclectic joining of North and South, Democrat and Republican—along with a healthy dash of Eastern Europe. Stuart G. Gibboney and Henry Alan Johnston were Virginians, both graduates of the University of Virginia Law School and both prominent New York City attorneys. Gibboney became the organization's first president; Johnston its secretary. Vice President Moses H. Grossman was a wealthy New York City judge, a man willing to put his money behind his beliefs. The first Board of Governor's included U.Va. President Dr. Edwin A. Alderman; Thomas E. Rush, president of the National Democratic Club; Charles D. Hilles, vice-chairman of the Republican National Committee; Virginia Governor E. Lee Trinkle, and New York City native Theodore Roosevelt. The first treasurer was Charles D. Makepeace, vice-president of the Seaboard National Bank.

Russian-born Jew Theodore "Fred" Kuper became Gibboney's general assistant—working almost as an advertising man—and subsequently served as the Foundation's lawyer. A native of Moscow, Fred Kuper later told Monticello curator James A. Bear, Jr. that he had "gotten off the boat at Ellis Island with only a bag in his hand." Kuper's zeal and creativity were put to good use during the organization's early years.

The Thomas Jefferson Memorial Foundation established its headquarters in New York at 115 Broadway (a building that by no coincidence also housed Judge Grossman's office and the Lawyers' Club). Office manager Jack Slaight had worked as a newspaper editor of *The New York World* and as Teddy Roosevelt's public relations advisor. A self-perpetuating board of nine directors was put in place to run the corporation, all other members comprised the Board of Governors, which acted in an advisory capacity. A constitution and a set of by-laws were drafted; educational and fund-raising committees were formed. But the most important task at hand, of course, was negotiating for the purchase of Jefferson's home from the ponderously-named Jefferson Monroe Levy.

Who was Jefferson M. Levy? How had he come to acquire what Littleton called Jefferson's "treasure house?" The story is jam-full of odd twists and turns, and plenty of fascinating characters. Jefferson M. Levy was the fourth private individual to own Monticello since it passed out of the Jefferson family's hands in 1831. In November of that year title to the property was conveyed to Charlottesville druggist James Turner Barclay who was interested in setting up a silkworm culture using Jefferson's mulberry trees. The experiment failed within a few years.

On May 20, 1836, Monticello was purchased by forty-four-year-old U.S. Navy Lieutenant Uriah Philips Levy. The Jewish gentleman admired Jefferson for his stance on religious freedom. Four years earlier Levy had written that Jefferson "did much to mold our Republic in a form in which a man's religion does not make him ineligible for political or governmental life." Levy spent a considerable amount of money repairing and maintaining Monticello. Uriah Levy died in 1862, leaving Jefferson's "little mountain" to the people of the United States. His intention was that Monticello be converted into an agricultural school for the orphaned sons of U.S. Navy warrant officers. As if anticipating problems, Levy's will stipulated two alternate benefactors: the Commonwealth of Virginia and the Hebrew congregations of New York, Philadelphia, and Richmond.

That same year—1862—the estate was seized by the Confederate States Government as alien property. Ironically, Jefferson's youngest grandchild, George Wythe Randolph, was Confederate States secretary of war at the time. On November 17, 1864, Monticello was sold to Benjamin F. Ficklin of Albemarle County. Ficklin was a V.M.I. graduate and one of the founders of the Pony Express. His ownership terminated at the end of hostilities, of course, as the property had been confiscated illegally.

The nation's woes subsided in 1865 but Monticello's were just beginning. During the war Levy's widow, and other heirs, had petitioned the New York State Supreme Court to declare the will null and void. The court ruled in their favor, saying the beneficiaries were not easily identifiable. The U.S. attorney general concurred. Now the problem was how to divide up Jefferson's property. To which of the Levy heirs did it belong? The Circuit Court of the City of Richmond decreed that the home, and 218 acres, be sold in order to settled the arguments over the will. When Monticello was finally sold on March 20, 1879—for $10,500—the purchaser was Jefferson Monroe Levy, Uriah Levy's nephew. The wealthy twenty-seven-year-old had previously assured his uncontested ownership by buying out most of the other claimants.

While Monticello's fate was being argued in the courts, the house and property—including the graveyard—had unfortunately fallen into an awful state of disrepair. Levy installed a new grounds superintendent and started the work of restoration. "Photographs of the pre-Levy period and those after his ownership," wrote Bear, "present conclusive evidence that his tenure was more than beneficial." Nonetheless, one of America's most historic homes soon became Levy's summer-season get-away. Levy family portraits and naval memorabilia were put on display.

As the nation started seriously contemplating its origins, individuals began inquiring after Thomas Jefferson's home. Visitation grew steadily. William Jennings Bryan offered to purchase the estate in 1897 but his overtures were rebuffed. Mrs. Littleton first visited Monticello in 1909 and found the experience very disappointing. "I had a heavy-hearted feeling," she wrote, "There was nothing of Jefferson. . . . He had dropped out and the Levy's had come. . . . Does [Levy] want a whole Nation crawling at his feet forever for permission to worship at this shrine of independence?" Littleton lobbied for purchase by the Federal Government but the movement failed. Levy was adamant about retaining the property. "When the White House is for sale," he declared, "then I will consider an offer for Monticello."

The recession that followed World War I, however, accomplished what Littleton could not. In 1919, because of financial losses, Jefferson Monroe Levy advertised Monticello, and 650 surrounding acres, for sale. The price was $400,000. Two other patriotic groups were organized in Richmond and Washington but were unable to come up with the money. Enter the Thomas Jefferson Memorial Foundation.

In January of 1923 Levy asked a friend to inform New York Judge Moses H. Grossman that he was hard pressed for money and forced to sell. Grossman had been in touch with the other associations and knew they would be willing to cooperate. Finally the timing was right for Monticello's preservation, and its preservation appeared to be on the minds of many. The American Institute of Architects noted, in a March 14, 1923 report: "The private ownership of Monticello continues to be regrettable: but much more so is the bad condition into which the house and especially the outbuildings have fallen. . . . [I]t is hoped that the efforts to purchase the house for the public may be prosecuted with greater success . . . and that the much needed work of maintenance and repair be undertaken at once."

Once formed the Thomas Jefferson Memorial Foundation went to work with a passion. Fred Kuper, during a trip to Richmond and Washington, was successful in bringing on board the other organizations. Gibboney, Makepeace, and Johnston were elected to an Executive Committee with the express purpose of negotiating with Jefferson M. Levy. But the seventy-one-year-old drove a hard bargain. "A number of conferences were held," wrote Bear, "before the 'best possible' terms were reached." The final price was $500,000: a payment of $100,000 in December 1923, at which point the title would exchange hands; a second payment of like sum; and the balance of $300,000 to be paid over a number of years with bonds of the Foundation, secured by a second mortgage. To seal the arrangement Gibboney and Grossman wrote personal checks to Levy totaling $10,000.

Now the problem was raising $90,000 in eight months. On April 23, 1923, Manny Strauss was elected chairman of the TJMF Ways and Means Committee. Meeting the first payment was Strauss's goal and several schemes to that affect were quickly announced. A "spiritual pilgrimage" from New York City to the "little mountain" was held in a stationary train parked in Grand Central Station. While movies were shown of an actual trip to Monticello, New York Senator Royal S. Copeland—dressed as a ticket agent—passed through the cars selling "tickets" at one cent a mile. The results were disappointing. Next an underwriter's program was adopted wherein Gibboney and Strauss procured promissory notes for amounts of $1,000—or multiples thereof.

In July, 1923, George G. Battle, chairman of the TJMF Finance Committee, told the newspapers that the Foundation's ultimate goal was one million dollars—half to acquire Jefferson's home and half to endow it. "He appealed to the nation to square its debt with the author of the Declaration," wrote historian Charles Hosmer, Jr., "hoping that Monticello would be an inspiration to the people, and a mirror of their gratitude. . . ." But the immediate debt was still short.

Strauss next organized a fund-raising, transcontinental speaking tour. Virginia Governor Trinkle and U.Va. President Alderman, and others, were to address audiences in twenty-five different cities. But, as it turned out, these men were far too busy. Kuper would have to do all the talking himself. So the diminutive lawyer "moved out across the West and South," wrote Hosmer, "speaking as many as seven times a day—often in areas very hostile to Jeffersonian ideas." Kuper developed a very effective speech using Jefferson's epitaph—"Author of the Declaration of American Independence, of the Statute of Virginia for Religious Freedom and Father of the University of Virginia"—to reveal how the statesman had thus defined America's loftiest principles: personal freedom, religious freedom, and education. But, recalled Kuper, "Jefferson did not open the purse strings of people with real money, even among people of modest means, he was a forgotten man."

When the $90,000 was paid in December, 1923, it was made up mostly of funds borrowed from banks on the basis of the pledges. Jefferson M. Levy cried during the ceremony in which the Thomas Jefferson Memorial Foundation took possession of Monticello. According to Kuper, Levy "said that he never dreamt he would ever part with the property." Jefferson M. Levy died the following March but his heiress held true to the terms of the agreement.

The Foundation now held title to Monticello, but the amount of money still owed was overwhelming. The task seemed insurmountable. A 1924 report to the American Institute of Architects warned, in fact, that should the Thomas Jefferson Memorial Foundation fail in its mission, it would be many years before another group would take up the challenge. But there were other challenges as well: the estate had to be supervised, and a visitation system had to be established. Gibboney and Kuper traveled to Monticello in order to begin the reorganization. The price of admission was set at fifty cents. Governor Trinkle, U.S. Senator Copeland, and President Alderman were appointed custodians to administer the property. Levy's superintendent was kept on but the Levy memorabilia was removed, much to the chagrin of the family.

Simultaneously, as part of its dual purpose of preservation and education, the Foundation began looking for ways to promote the "basic democratic ideals which [Jefferson] served and championed." But in the early 1920s there were no new biographies of Jefferson. And the textbooks mentioned him merely as president and author of the Declaration. "For these reasons," wrote Kuper, "we planned to direct the campaign on an educational basis through the children and their teachers. . . ."

The Foundation's programs over the next few years consisted mainly of special events. These "publicity stunts" raised money but also raised the public awareness of Jefferson and his life. Jefferson's birthday celebrations, for example, were inaugurated in public schools, the accumulated "gifts" going toward the preservation of the property. "We hope the people in every State of the Union will respond generously to our appeal," stated Gibboney in the March 12, 1924 issue of *The World*, "and make certain the early completion of the purchase fund." New York Governor Alfred E. Smith was the first of many officials to set aside April 6 to 13 as "Jefferson Week." The Foundation provided free transportation from New York City to Monticello on the actual birthday. Fifty boys and girls toured the home and the university, all the while taking notes from the information presented by the guides.

The Foundation moved forward on other fronts as well. U.Va. architecture professor Fiske Kimball was made chairman of the Monticello Restoration Committee in 1924. The long-time director of the Philadelphia Museum of Art was the perfect man for the job. Eminently knowledgeable on Jefferson's career as an amateur architect, Kimball—as member of the Preservation Committee of the American Institute of Architects—had long supported the movement to purchase and preserve the property. *The World* reported in 1925 that Kimball hoped "not only to restore the lawns and gardens . . . but also to return to the historic mansion much of the furniture bought by the author of the Declaration. . . ." In these endeavors Kimball was successful and even acquired Jefferson pieces from some of the ex-president's descendants. Kimball continued to serve Monticello until 1954.

As the hundredth anniversary of Jefferson's death on July 4, 1826 approached, a Centennial Committee was set up to organize an observance. The committee conducted an election in which the candidates—all young ladies—who received 50,000 votes would win a July, 1926 trip to Paris. The "votes" cost ten cents, so the ladies each needed to raise $5,000 to win. "Kuper arranged the tours in France to be educational," wrote Hosmer, "especially from the standpoint of democratic ideals." Complaints were voiced against an election where the "votes" were purchased but *The New York Times* strongly supported the idea. Fifty-eight girls toured France as a result of a campaign that netted over $300,000 for Monticello.

The year 1926 saw several other special events staged by the Foundation. On February 17 all of New York City's school children rose and repeated the Foundation's "Patriot's Pledge of Faith"—a pledge to the "fundamental ideals" set forth in the Declaration. "And . . . as an evidence of my gratitude for the blessings which that immortal document has assured . . ." it concludes, "I do hereby make this contribution for the preservation of Monticello . . . as a National Memorial to the Author of the Declaration of Independence and as a Patriotic Shrine for the Children of America." The youngsters of New York City thus donated $34,864.

For the one hundred and fiftieth anniversary celebration of the signing of the Declaration one of Jefferson's carriages was driven from Charlottesville to Philadelphia in a reenactment of his historic 1776 trip. Thomas Jefferson Randolph IV—the "Sage of Monticello's" great, great grandson—wrote a letter to the Foundation authenticating the vehicle as his ancestor's "one-horse gig." (It was actually a two-horse phaeton that Jefferson had designed in 1805.) Representatives from various American cities joined the procession, which made a brief stop-over in Washington so that President Calvin Coolidge could make a donation.

Through the staging of these, and other, campaigns the Thomas Jefferson Memorial Foundation was able to announce—in the September 22, 1928 issue of the *New York Herald*—that only $28,500 of the debt remained. The Great Depression caused the Foundation to cut back staff and hugely affected its ability to retire the debt. The last payments were made in 1940. But those first few years were the most important. In negotiating with Jefferson M. Levy and raising what were then astronomical amounts of money the Thomas Jefferson Memorial Foundation accomplished what Hosmer called a "stupendous task." And they brought the "Sage of Monticello" a portion of his rightful due. The Foundation was determined, wrote Bear, "to popularize Jefferson and make Monticello a national shrine; here they were eminently successful." These goals were achieved with perseverance, and no little dab of creativity. "So you see we had plenty of 'corny stunts,'" remembered Kuper in 1971, "But Monticello was saved!"

BIBLIOGRAPHY

Herbert B. Adams, *Thomas Jefferson and the University of Virginia* (Washington, 1888).

Stephen E. Ambrose, *Undaunted Courage: Meriwether Lewis, Thomas Jefferson, and the Opening of the American West* (New York, 1996).

Thomas Anburey, *Travels Through the Interior Parts of America In a Series of Letters* (London, 1789).

George W. Bagby, *The Old Virginia Gentleman and Other Sketches* (New York, 1910).

James A. Bear, *Jefferson at Monticello* (Charlottesville, 1967).

William L. Beiswanger, Peter J. Hatch, Lucia Stanton, and Susan R. Stein, *Thomas Jefferson's Monticello* (Charlottesville, 2002).

Guy Meriwether Benson, *Exploring the West from Monticello: A Perspective in Maps from Columbus to Lewis and Clark* (Charlottesville, 1995).

Rebecca Bowman, "Jefferson, Neology, and Jurisprudence," *Spring Dinner at Monticello, April 12, 1998* (Charlottesville, 1998).

Jacques Pierre Brissot, *New Travels in the United States of America, 1788* (Cambridge, 1964).

Philip Alexander Bruce, *History of the University of Virginia, 1819–1919* (New York, 1920–22) 5 volumes.

Andrew Burnaby, *Travels Through the Middle Settlements in North America* (New York, 1970).

David I. Bushnell Jr., "The Five Monacan Towns in Virginia, 1607," *Smithsonian Miscellaneous Collections* (Washington, 1937).

John Edwards Caldwell, *A Tour Through Part of Virginia in the Summer of 1808* (Richmond, 1851).

Charlottesville 200th Anniversary Commission, "Charlottesville 1762—1962" (Charlottesville, 1962).

Maj. Gen. Marquis de Chastellux, *Travels in North-America in the Years 1780—81—82* (New York, 1827).

Noble E. Cunningham, Jr., *In Pursuit of Reason: The Life of Thomas Jefferson* (New York, 1987).

Virginius Dabney, *Mr. Jefferson's University, a History* (Charlottesville, 1981).

_____, *Virginia, The New Dominion: A History from 1607 to the Present* (New York, 1971).

Bernard DeVoto, editor, *The Journals of Lewis and Clark* (Boston, 1997).

David Hackett Fischer and James C. Kelly, *Bound Away: Virginia and the Westward Movement* (Charlottesville, 2000).

Dan L. Flores, *Jefferson and Southwest Exploration* (Norman, Oklahoma, 1984).

Bryan Clark Green, Calder Loth, and William M.S. Rasmussen, *Lost Virginia: Vanished Architecture of the Old Dominion* (Charlottesville, 2001).

Desmond Guinness, *Mr. Jefferson, Architect* (New York, 1973).

John H. Gwathmey, *Twelve Virginia Counties: Where the Western Migration Began* (Richmond, 1937).

Pendleton Hogan, *The Lawn: A Guide to Jefferson's University* (Charlottesville, 1987).

Charles B. Hosmer, Jr., *The Presence of the Past: A History of the Preservation Movement in the United States before Williamsburg* (New York, 1965).

Donald Jackson, *Thomas Jefferson and the Stony Mountains: Exploring the West from Monticello* (Urbana, Illinois, 1979).

Thomas Jefferson, *Notes on the State of Virginia* (Chapel Hill, 1954).

_____, *The Autobiography of Thomas Jefferson, 1743–1790* (Philadelphia, 2005).

Willard Rouse Jillson, *Big Bone Lick: An Outline of its History, Geology, and Paleontology* (Louisville, 1936).

K. Edward Lay, *The Architecture of Jefferson Country: Charlottesville and Albemarle County, Virginia* (Charlottesville, 2000).

Henry "Light Horse Harry" Lee, *The American Revolution in the South* (New York, 1969).

Maud Littleton, *One Wish* (New York, 1912).

J. Jefferson Looney, "Thomas Jefferson: Practical Scientist," *Journal of the Pennsylvania Academy of Science* 67(2), 1993.

Dumas Malone, *Jefferson the Virginian* (Boston, 1948).

_____, *Jefferson and the Rights of Man* (Boston, 1951).

_____, *Jefferson and the Ordeal of Liberty* (Boston, 1962).

_____, *Jefferson the President: First Term, 1801–1805* (Boston, 1970).

_____, *Jefferson the President: Second Term, 1805–1809* (Boston, 1974).

_____, *Jefferson and His Time: The Sage of Monticello* (Boston, 1981).

Edwin T. Martin, *Thomas Jefferson: Scientist* (New York, 1952).

Ben C. McCary, *Indians in Seventeenth-Century Virginia* (Charlottesville, 1957).

Samuel L. Mitchill, *A Discourse on the Character and Services of Thomas Jefferson* (Charlottesville, 1982).

John Hammond Moore, *Albemarle: Jefferson's County, 1727–1976* (Charlottesville, 1976).

John S. Patton, *Jefferson, Cabell and the University of Virginia* (New York, 1906).

Henry S. Randall, *The Life of Thomas Jefferson* (Philadelphia, 1865).

Sarah N. Randolph, *The Domestic Life of Thomas Jefferson* (Charlottesville, 1939).

Mary Rawlings, *The Albemarle of Other Days* (Charlottesville, 1925).

Howard C. Rice, Jr., "Jefferson's Gift of Fossils to the Museum of Natural History in Paris," *Proceedings of the American Philosophical Society*, vol. 95, no. 6 (December 1951).

Eudora Ramsay Richardson, *Jefferson's Albemarle: A Guide to Albemarle County and the City of Charlottesville, Virginia* (Charlottesville, 1941).

James P. Ronda, *Finding the West: Explorations with Lewis and Clark* (Albuquerque, 2001).

_____, *Jefferson's West: A Journey with Lewis and Clark* (Charlottesville, 200).

Emily J. Salmon and Edward D. C. Campbell, Jr., Editors, *The Hornbook of Virginia History: A Ready-Reference Guide to the Old Dominion's People, Places, and Past* (Richmond, 1994).

John Rennie Short, *Representing the Republic: Mapping the United States, 1600–1900* (London, 2001).

C. Bernard Shultz, "Nebraska's Fossil Elephants: The Mastodonts and Mammoths," *University of Nebraska, Lincoln News*, vol. 54, no. 6 (September 1974).

Lucia Stanton, *Free Some Day: The African-American Families of Monticello* (Charlottesville, 2000).

_____, *Slavery at Monticello* (Charlottesville, 1996).

Banastre Tarleton, *A History of the Campaign of 1780 and 1781 in the southern provinces of North America* (Dublin, 1786).

Carl Newton Tyson, *The Red River in Southwestern History* (Norman, Oklahoma, 1981).

Dr. Alan Williams, *The Road to Independence: Virginia 1763–1783* (Richmond, 1976).

Rev. Edgar Woods, *History of Albemarle County in Virginia: Giving some account of what it was by nature, of what it was made by man, and of some of the men who made it* (Charlottesville, 1901).

ABOUT THE AUTHOR

Rick Britton is a central Virginia-based author, historian, and cartographer. A native of Richmond, Virginia, he spent many of his formative years abroad. When Rick lived near Buenos Aires, Argentina, a beloved uncle, Renato Romano, was fond of regaling him with wonderful stories about the many great Virginians—Robert E. Lee, "Stonewall" Jackson, George Washington, and of course Thomas Jefferson. Back home in Richmond, Rick's paternal grandmother began buying him Civil War books as soon as he could read. Rick grew up loving Virginia history.

Rick Britton has been writing about Virginia's fascinating past since the mid-1990s. An award-winning historical journalist, his work has appeared in the pages of the *Richmond Times Dispatch*, the *Washington Times*, the *Fredericksburg Freelance-Star*, *Civil War Magazine*, *Civil War Times Illustrated*, *Virginia*, the *U.Va. Alumni News*, and *Albemarle Magazine* (where he served for over six years as contributing editor). Having published over 200 articles—most of them on the history of the Old Dominion—Rick Britton is the current editor of *The Magazine of Albemarle County History*. His first book, *Albemarle & Charlottesville: An Illustrated History of the First 150 Years* (published in 2006 by the Albemarle Charlottesville Historical Society), was well-received and quickly sold out.

Because of his writing career, Rick is frequently called upon to present lectures and talks. He also gives tours of many of Virginia's historic sites and hallowed battlefields. And he is a well-published cartographer, or map artist—having illustrated the maps for literally dozens of history books—as well as a regular weekly guest on WINA's "Charlottesville, Right Now" radio show, hosted by Coy Barefoot. Rick Britton resides in Charlottesville with his wife, and two rather large felines.

INDEX

Page numbers in italics refer to images.

Breinigsville, PA USA
25 September 2009
224727BV00003B/2/P